3-D

SALES

Leela,

Share with Passion!

ERIK THERWANGER

3-D
SALES

Change Your Perception of Selling and
Experience New Levels of Success

Published in Agoura Hills, California, by Think GREAT® LLC

3-D Sales™ is a trademark of Think GREAT® LLC

The GOAL Formula™ is a trademark of Think GREAT® LLC

Think GREAT® is a registered trademark of Think GREAT® LLC

ISBN 978-0-9840858-2-8

BISAC Subject Headings:

BUS058010 – BUSINESS & ECONOMICS / Sales & Selling / Management

3DS_Book_v01u – 07/01/11

Dedicated to:

Everyone who told me 'no' throughout my sales journey. My desire to earn your 'yes' has transformed me into a 3–Dimensional Sales Leader.

Everyone who has purchased this book. I have earned your 'yes' and you have begun your own 3–D transformation.

Everyone who has found themselves in sales and is looking to find themselves in sales! Your desire to change your perception about selling, enhance your sales results, and improve your life in the process, has made this book a reality.

The amazing sales professionals whom I have had the honor of working with; your unselfish ability to teach me the ropes, about sales and myself, has forever changed my life.

CONTENTS

INTRODUCTION

SEE DIFFERENT RESULTS

A new perception of sales.

Most people who sell for a living never anticipated being in sales. As children, we share dreams of becoming doctors, lawyers, actors, singers, business owners, or professional athletes. Not one of my childhood friends ever said, "When I grow up I want to sell..." insurance, used cars, cell phones, or anything for that matter. In high school, I would have been voted 'Least Likely to Sell', if that category even existed in our yearbooks.

Sales is not the dream career people typically strive for. As a child, I loved going to the movies with my father. I grew up on Indiana Jones, Star Wars, and all of the great '80s action films. In high school, I not only had the dream of becoming a filmmaker, but I had a plan. I had always wanted to serve our country so I made the decision to enlist in the armed services, complete my tour of duty, and use the G.I. Bill to go to film school. The idea of selling was not part of my dream or my plan to get there.

But sometimes, life has a unique way of guiding us into the path of unlimited possibilities and greater achievements. Three weeks after turning eighteen, my status changed from civilian to recruit as I began the rigorous training known as *boot camp*. Four tough–as–nails drill instructors led my platoon through intense physical challenges and demanding mental conditioning. Their non–stop, in–your–face training techniques did more than just help us to complete basic training, it forged us into U.S. Marines.

I completed my four year tour of duty and was honorably discharged, just after the first Gulf War had ended. I was still deeply focused on becoming a filmmaker so I packed away my combat boots and camouflage pants and I enrolled in college. It felt great to be on the path to my dreams. After completing my Associates Degree at Orange Coast College, I began the Cinema/Television program at the University of Southern California.

By the end of 1998, I had been a civilian for nearly eight years and was working in the entertainment industry. On Halloween of that year, I married my sweetheart, Gina. We had an amazing wedding, complete with a costume party reception. Gina and I were excited to start our life together and to accomplish the wonderful goals we had set. We wanted to buy a home, start a family, and travel all over the world. Life was great and getting better every day.

The following summer, Gina threw me an amazing surprise party to celebrate my 30th birthday. It was obvious that she had put in a great deal of effort because I remember her being unusually tired that day. But she had pulled it off and I celebrated into the night with family and friends. Although the party was a complete surprise, it paled in comparison to the surprise I received the next day.

Do you remember the moment that your career began heading in the direction of sales? I certainly do. I absolutely loved my *non-sales* position in the entertainment industry and had just started working with a new company when my phone rang. It was Gina. She was crying, which made it difficult to understand what she was saying. But three words registered with absolute clarity. Those three words would change our lives forever. I will never forget the sound of her voice as she said, "I have cancer."

Neither my new job nor my dream of becoming a filmmaker mattered to me. I was now my wife's caregiver and her health was my only concern. The next few days seemed like a blur as I took her to doctor appointments to meet with different specialists. When her final diagnosis came in, it was not good. She had Non-Hodgkin's Lymphoma and we were told that it was very aggressive. Her oncologist immediately scheduled her first cycle of chemotherapy.

After we received a quick overview about her treatments, I tried to notify our family and friends of what was going on. What was going on? I didn't exactly know. I just knew that a lot was going on and I did not know what to do next. I was not aware yet, but my career path was being guided in a new direction.

Our one–year anniversary was just around the corner and what was once our bright future seemed over–shadowed by our dark present. Each day, things seemed farther and farther out of my control. It is difficult to find the words to truly express the amount of fear we were living with, but it was more than either of us had ever encountered.

As Gina began her first chemotherapy session, we were advised that she would lose her hair and become violently ill as the chemicals took effect. After each treatment, she would be sick for about two weeks before starting to feel better. On the third week, she would receive the next dose of 'chemo' and the cycle would start all over again. Gina was scheduled for seven of these treatments.

I watched helplessly as her nurses prepared her for the first treatment. Then her oncologist pulled me aside and told me something that would become the foundation of how I approached my new role as Gina's caregiver. In fact, it has become the foundation of how I perceive my sales career. With absolute certainty he said, "Keep her thinking positive, no matter what you hear or see. It will help her to fight back." Well, I had my orders. I finally had something that I could control!

I drove Gina back to our small apartment, keeping the doctors words at the forefront of my thoughts. Just like they said, she became ill by the time we got home. As I wiped her forehead with a damp cloth to comfort her, she cried and told me that she felt like she was going to die. I knew that now was the time to follow my orders, but it was challenging to keep her positive during all of this.

In addition to the stress of having cancer, I knew that our financial situation would be heavily on her mind. Unable to work, Gina was immediately placed on disability. I was not making much money at my new job and it was only a matter of time until the effects of our finances would soon be felt. With everything she was going through, I had to make sure that she was not worried about our financial situation too.

As Gina's condition worsened, I took more time off from my new job. As understanding as my boss was, I knew it was impractical to think that I could stay employed there. In the midst of Gina's battle with cancer, I searched for a way to make money and control my schedule, but my options were limited.

I discovered an opportunity to do both in the financial services industry. Although it only required me to pass a few tests and get licensed, it did involve the one thing I never wanted to do – sell. But Gina's condition was my number one priority, so I pushed aside my hang–ups about selling and made a commitment to make this 'sales thing' work.

With four years of military training, eight years in the entertainment industry, and absolutely not one single second of sales experience, I started my new career – in sales! As long as I could pay the bills and have time with my wife, then call me a salesman! Being in sales was foreign to me, but I had a lot at stake.

My position did not pay a salary. Instead, I would earn money solely through commissions. I did not have a background in the financial services industry, nor did I use the products I would be selling. I did not own a home, have a life insurance policy, or have any of the investments I would be offering. I was also not what you would consider your *typical* sales guy and I certainly did not fit the mold of a salesman.

Although I lacked any formal training, or even the slightest desire to sell, I was about to enter into the unfamiliar, uncomfortable, and often unforgiving world of sales. I was stepping out onto a high–wire without a net and the odds seemed to be stacked against me. If I was going to successfully make it to the other side, I would need an edge.

Like most sales associates who want to increase their sales, I naturally focused on improving my sales skills and increasing my knowledge of products and services. Although I polished my skills, they did not necessarily translate into more commissions. My sales results did not improve just because my sales skills improved. My sales results improved because my perception of sales changed. The more depth I added to my sales performance, the more results I experienced.

THE BENEFITS OF BECOMING 3-DIMENSIONAL

I started my sales career during extremely challenging times, but I was determined to experience new levels of success. During my transformation from a salesperson to a 3-Dimensional Sales Leader, I discovered more than just sales skills; I discovered my true potential. More importantly than learning *how* to sell, I learned *why* to sell.

Despite Gina's first battle with cancer, I went on to become a top producer, recruiter, and trainer in the financial services industry. I later took my 3-dimensional sales skills back into the entertainment industry and became the vice president of a post-production company. I recruited and trained a sales team that would generate over $25,000,000 in sales.

I never intended for my career path to head in the direction of sales, but my entire life has been elevated to new levels because I transformed myself into a 3-Dimensional Sales Leader. In fact, my sales journey has not only helped me to define new dreams, it has allowed me to understand my greater purpose – to help people to accomplish their goals, no matter what circumstances they face. That purpose has led to the creation of my company, Think GREAT.

Although I never imagined having a career in sales, I now train sales professionals across the country on the ground-breaking techniques in this book. *3–D Sales* is more than just a detailed account of the techniques and strategies I used during my personal sales journey; it is your unwavering guide to adding a new dimension to your sales performance.

By reading *3–D Sales* you will:

- Learn the *3 Ds of Selling: Desire – Determination – Decisions*
- Understand how to *Keep Your Sales Gears Turning*
- Discover that *The More You Know, the More You Grow*

Regardless of your circumstances, you can always add more depth to your sales performance and experience greater success. I know this because tough times did not end with Gina's first battle with cancer. She would be diagnosed two more times, her most recent bout with breast cancer was at the end of 2010.

In addition to surviving her battles with cancer, she now helps me to run our company. During all three of her bouts with this disease, I have been in sales. Our circumstances have not always been optimal for building a successful sales career, but no one's ever are. Despite our challenges, I have focused on being a 3–Dimensional Sales Leader and I have achieved great levels of success. You can too!

Packed with inspirational stories, essential sales strategies, and proven techniques, *3–D Sales* is for anyone who wants to improve their personal sales results and/or their team results. The foundation of *3–D Sales* will allow you, your team members, and your organization to experience new levels of success. *3–D Sales* will inspire you to take action, empower you to make an impact, and transform you into a successful 3–Dimensional Sales Leader who achieves greater results. Are you ready to experience new levels of success in your sales career? How about in your life? *3–D Sales* will open your eyes to a revolutionary new way of selling.

Think GREAT,

Erik

PART I

BECOMING 3-DIMENSIONAL

PART I

BECOMING 3–DIMENSIONAL

How do you want your clients to perceive you?

Having a dream career, enjoying an amazing lifestyle, and having more free time are usually enough to entice most people to try their hand in sales. Everyone will attempt to sell something at some point in their lives. Hopeful entrepreneurs try their hands at in–home businesses, join network marketing companies, or find themselves making hundreds of phone calls as a telemarketer. Some acquire licenses to sell products as independent contractors while others make lateral moves within their company to enter into a sales department.

Individual reasons and situations vary, but almost everyone is willing to do whatever it takes to achieve a greater life – even if it means selling! Although many try, very few experience the results they dreamed of. In fact, most fail to even achieve mediocre results in their new ventures. Unfortunately, bad experiences are all too common and the majority of sales careers are shorter lived than a Hollywood marriage!

Failing at sales opportunities often leaves people with a bad taste about sales and salespeople. Because most everyone tries sales, and many fail, it is safe to say that you will probably sell to someone who has tried sales, failed, and has a negative perception about it. To succeed at selling, it is your job to positively enhance your clients' perception about sales and salespeople. Therefore, changing your view about sales will be necessary before you can change theirs.

Selling is a lot like art. It has very little to do with the raw materials: paint, marble, or clay. It has little to do with the tools: brushes, pencils, or chisels. It has everything to do with the vision of the artist and his/her ability to successfully apply the materials and tools to create the final picture. Too many salespeople focus only on their materials and their tools. They fail to utilize the resources available to create their sales masterpiece.

Sir Isaac Newton once said, "I was like a boy playing on the sea-shore, and diverting myself now and then finding a smoother pebble or a prettier shell than ordinary, while the great ocean of truth lay all undiscovered before me." Most people diligently search for the little sales *treasures* that will enhance their careers and change their results, but they often over-look the *ocean of opportunity* in front of them.

The extent of your success is always determined by what sales dimension you are operating in. What are the different dimensions, you ask? Great question! Let's take a closer look at each dimension. Try to identify the one you sell in.

The 3 Sales Dimensions:

> 1-Dimensional Sales – make a buck
>
> 2-Dimensional Sales – make a living
>
> 3-Dimensional Sales – make an impact

Do you want your clients or prospects to view you as 1-dimensional or 2-dimensional? Of course not, especially when 3-dimensional is an option.

Statistics vary, but most salespeople quit before making their first sale. Roughly 90% of salespeople are unable to generate income and fail to even reach the first dimension – making a buck. By focusing on basic sales skills, some eager hopefuls are able to earn some money by becoming 1-dimensional. Others continue to learn new techniques and strategies and develop 2–dimensional capabilities, making positive enhancements in their business and in their lifestyle.

But a select few focus on something greater. They take their sales abilities to a level that impacts the lives of those around them, not just their own. 3–Dimensional Sales Leaders have a unique perception that ushers in greater levels of success. Becoming 3–dimensional does not happen by chance, it happens by choice.

1–DIMENSIONAL SALES

Those who operate in the first dimension are able to earn some money despite their lack of any formal sales training. They usually experience a higher level of rejection, but the occasional 'yes' is enough to keep them selling. Is this you?

The Traits of 1–Dimensional Salespeople:
- Possess an average ability to explain products and services
- Focus on their results
- Develop strong leads
- Show excitement

1–dimensional salespeople often feel like they are running in circles to grow their business.

2–DIMENSIONAL SALES

Those who operate in the second dimension are able to earn enough money to make a living. They experience fewer rejections and are able to develop some key clients and referrals. The occasional 'no' causes them to focus on increasing their professionalism. They recruit others into sales to build their sales teams and share in the income produced by these teams. I refer to them as sales professionals rather than salespeople. Is this you?

The Traits of 2-Dimensional Sales Professionals:

- Display an above average ability to explain products and services
- Focus on their goals
- Develop key clients
- Show excitement and drive

2-dimensional sales professionals often feel like they are running on a treadmill to grow their business.

3-DIMENSIONAL SALES

Those who operate in the third dimension are able to make a difference in the lives around them, which in turn makes a significant difference in their own lives. They help others to thrive and experience little to no rejection. The infrequent 'no' is perceived merely as the first two letters of 'not yet'. They expand upon their own dreams and encourage others to pursue their dreams. They tend to build and lead dedicated teams to great success. Could this be you?

The Traits of 3-Dimensional Sales Leaders:

- Have a keen ability to present the benefits of their products and services
- Focus on their clients' goals
- Develop powerful relationships
- Show excitement, drive, and certainty

3-Dimensional Sales Leaders are in control, moving in the right direction to accomplish their sales goals by helping their team members and clients reach their own goals.

BECOMING 3-DIMENSIONAL

Anyone can become 3-dimensional in sales. You are not limited by age, gender, or ethnicity. Some careers, like sports, the military, police work, or being a fire fighter may require specific physical abilities to excel, but 3-dimensional selling does not rely on your physical strength. In fact, there are no external parameters to becoming 3-dimensional. You already possess everything you need internally.

The 3 Ds of Selling:

- Desire
- Determination
- Decisions

Having a strong desire will help you to create a crystal-clear vision of what you need. Exhibiting a powerful determination will enhance your ability to stay on course with your goals. Making great decisions will open up opportunities to create the career you dream about. Becoming a 3-Dimensional Sales Leader is about understanding these three elements and infusing their unique benefits into every aspect of your sales efforts.

You have probably noticed in these first few pages that I refer to salespeople who operate in the third dimension as 3-Dimensional Sales Leaders. Selling is not a sales position, it is a leadership position. Leadership must be the foundation of your sales career. Your clients will not follow a follower, but they will follow a leader.

Throughout this book, I will promote key leadership principles that I learned as a U.S. Marine. These *A Leader's Perspectives* will give you an advantage in sales, unlike anything you have experienced before.

A Leader's Perspective

Every action you take, do it as a leader!

A BOOK WITH A GOAL

3-D Sales is not about adding to what you have to sell, it is about multiplying what you have to offer. By applying the concepts of this book, you will enhance your sales performance and stay on track to achieve the sales goals required to experience new levels of success. The ultimate goal of *3-D Sales* is to provide beginners with a head start and experts with a new dimension for success. Divided into three powerful sections, this book pays careful attention to the attitudes and actions necessary to get the sales results you desire.

Part I: Becoming 3-Dimensional – Teaches you how to change your perception of yourself, your clients, and your success in sales by focusing on the 3 Ds of Selling: Desire, Determination, and Decisions.

Part II: Keep Your Sales Gears Turning – Identifies the five basic gears needed to keep your sales machine operating smoothly, which will allow you to properly develop new prospects, maintain existing clients, and get referrals.

Part III: The More You Know, The More You Grow – Shows you that sales is not a numbers game, it is a knowledge game, won by those who ask 3-dimensional questions.

As a 3-Dimensional Sales Leader, I changed my perception of selling, experienced a new level of success in sales, and achieved a greater life. I dramatically increased my income, bought my first home, purchased rental properties, wrote several books, defined my greater purpose, and launched my company – Think GREAT.

Given the choice between working with a sales representative who is focused only on their payout or working with a sales representative who is focused on a client's best interests, whom would you choose? Exactly! So would your clients. People like to be around and buy from a person whom they can trust to perform for them.

Are you ready to become a 3–Dimensional Sales Leader?

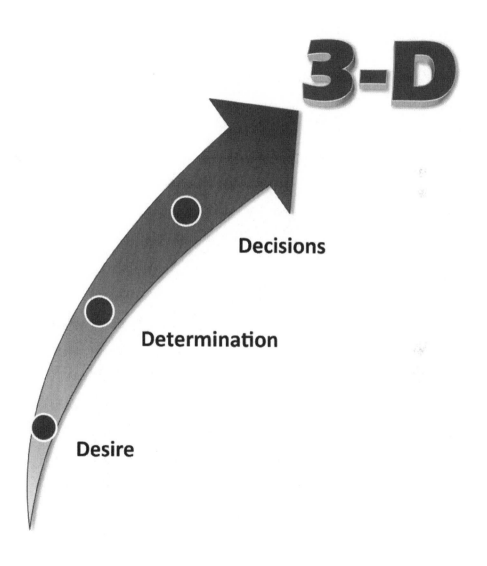

Chapter 1

Desire

...must be deeper than your paycheck.

Being a salesperson is a lot like being a professional athlete. While both fields have the potential for an amazing income, the best salespeople and athletes focus on more than just money. Having the desire to win, they are willing to do what it takes to accomplish their goal. Although most superstars typically do not have a desire to practice, they do possess a strong desire to win. Football players desire to win the Super Bowl. Baseball players desire to win the World Series. Olympians desire to win the gold medal.

Most salespeople desire to win, too. They desire what a successful sales career will bring them: lifestyle, security, freedom, etc. Many people do not have a desire to sell. This is not a bad thing. It is a reality. People get excited to close big sales and understandably so, but that is not what they are truly passionate about. Passion is always deeper than a paycheck. If the depth of your desire does not exceed your wallet, it is highly unlikely that your earnings will ever exceed your expectations.

I have seen people get excited when they make a big sale or when they lock in a high-volume client. And I have seen the spark in their eyes when they receive valuable referrals. That is excitement! But that excitement would quickly fade if there was no financial gain. Why? True desire is not about money.

Many people struggle in sales because they confuse excitement with desire. Your desires represent the things in life you are passionate about.

Those with the greatest results focus on much more than just their commissions.

To succeed in sales, you must be able to distinguish between excitement and desire. A successful sales career must have a high level of excitement while a 3–dimensional sales career must also have a high level of desire. People get excited about the money they earn because it brings them closer to their desires – their goals.

STRONG DESIRES

Having strong desires will do little to help your sales efforts, unless you are able to transform them into realities. Successful salespeople set and accomplish sales goals, turning their desires into achievements. Writing your goals down will create a sense of urgency and validate the importance of your desires. Strong desires create a strong commitment level. If your goals stay in your head, they cannot become results.

Gina and I were facing many adversities when setting the goal of buying our first home. My desire to keep her attitude positive by purchasing that home made me take a closer look at how to accomplish our goals. Regardless of our difficult circumstances, I needed a solid plan to set our goals, stay on track, and ensure that we accomplished them.

Combining my training in the U.S. Marine Corps with my duties as Gina's caregiver, I developed a detailed plan to accomplish any goal, big or small, personal or professional, no matter what circumstances we faced. I wrote the book, *The GOAL Formula*, which describes the necessary steps to accomplish life–changing goals and turn your desires into realities.

The acronym G.R.E.A.T. illustrates the first element of *The GOAL Formula*.

The 5 Steps to Accomplishing Goals:

1. **G**oals – Identify important Goals in your life
2. **R**easons – Establish powerful Reasons for accomplishing your goals
3. **E**xpectations – Set high Expectations for yourself
4. **A**ctions – Take all of the Actions necessary to achieve your goals
5. **T**racking – Track your results systematically

You will be more successful in accomplishing your goals by combining these steps with two other elements: time and people. When you concentrate your efforts in a well–defined block of time and enlist the support of others, you will set and accomplish short–term and long–term goals, increase your sales performance, and experience new levels of success.

I cannot overstate the importance of goals to a 3–Dimensional Sales Leader. Yes, they will help to transform your desires into realities, but accomplishing your goals is only half of the scenario. You are not the only one with desires. Your clients have them too. Helping them to accomplish their goals will help you to obtain your results.

For more information on *The GOAL Formula*, visit my website: www.thinkgreat90.com

UNDERSTANDING SALES

Selling is a natural part of any job. Doctors, lawyers, athletes, politicians, filmmakers, and employees are selling every day. They may not consider themselves sales professionals, but their success is based on their ability to influence people to buy what they offer. Your success will be based on your ability to influence your buyers.

Doctors want to attract more patients. Lawyers want to gain more clients. Athletes want to sell more jerseys. Politicians want to lock in more votes.

Filmmakers want to sell more tickets. Employees want to earn more promotions. You are no different. You have something to offer, and there are potential buyers out there. You want them to choose you as their sales representative.

By choosing a career in sales, you will dramatically increase your ability to accomplish your goals. It is an amazing vehicle that will help you to reach your ultimate destination – your desires. But you must understand how your 'sales vehicle' operates in order to achieve the best performance.

Developing a clear definition of sales is essential to achieving your desires. Trust me, any potential client already has a definition of it, and it may not match yours. Your perception about sales is your definition of sales. To enhance your perception, let's take a closer look at the true meaning of sales.

The Common Definition of Sales:

> **SALES** [seylz] –noun *plural* : the act of selling; *specifically* : the exchange of goods or services for an amount of money or its equivalent –adjective : of, pertaining to, or engaged in sales.

By this definition, everyone who works is selling. Every employee is in sales: part–timers, full–timers, managers, supervisors, and executive leaders. People exchange their services for a paycheck. In essence, they 'sell' their company on keeping them employed and promoting them. Employees sell themselves through their performance, proficiency, results, initiative, customer service, etc. Those who fail to sell their company on keeping them could be looking for a new job.

On the other hand, business owners 'sell' their employees on staying. Businesses offer benefits, competitive pay, great working environments, opportunities for growth, etc. Businesses that fail to sell their employees on staying could be looking for new employees.

For those of us in the sales profession, our livelihood depends on our ability to also sell outside the confines of our business. We sell products, services, or perhaps a combination of both. We sell on an *external* basis and our perception of sales must influence people beyond the walls of our office.

In the financial services industry, I sold products such as life insurance, mutual funds, and education plans. I also offered services such as asset management, debt elimination, and financial profiles. In the entertainment industry, I sold products such as DVD replication, high definition duplication, and closed captioning. I also offered services such as media vaulting, digital delivery, and quality assurance.

I have to admit that I was not overly excited by any of the items I sold. But I did have the strong desire to offer my clients something of value; something that made their lives better. When you successfully sell to someone, you have the ability to enhance their life. In fact, the product or service that they purchase from you could be life–changing.

> **A Leader's Perspective** You do not have to be passionate about the products you are selling to passionately sell them.

Even if you sell items that may not seem life–changing, you may be helping that person to do their job better; making their lives better to some degree. Be proud to be in sales. The work you do can change many lives, including your own. Sales is the vehicle we use to achieve our desires. Now that you have a 3–dimensional perception of sales, it is time to put the 'pedal to the metal', and get your vehicle moving in the right direction!

STAY FOCUSED ON YOUR DESIRES

Strengthening your sales efforts by focusing on your desires is like adding high–performance fuel to your engine. Most salespeople fill up their tank, push the gas pedal, and speed off in their new sales career. But as soon as they take their eyes off of their desires, they spin out of control. That is why so many sales careers crash and burn. To stay in control of your sales results, stay focused on your desires.

Desire rarely involves just one person. When you are passionate about something, it often touches the lives of others. Remember, becoming 3–dimensional is about making a difference in the lives of others, not just in your own life! Most salespeople have the desire of creating financial security, developing a great lifestyle, and having more free time. Yet, I have never met anyone who aimed at these goals, only to enjoy them alone.

During her first battle with cancer, Gina and I shared the powerful desire of buying our first home. We lived in a small, two–bedroom apartment, and Gina dreamed of decorating our own home. She wanted a backyard for my sons, a dining room to entertain our guests, and a romantic fire-place for the two of us. Talking about our new home always raised her spirits, but I knew that the excitement of owning a home would fizzle, if I did not make it a reality.

Unfortunately, my sales efforts were not paying off yet. Instead, our time was occupied with doctor appointments, hospital visits, and complica-tions from Gina's treatments. Buying a home did not seem possible, but our desire remained strong. We stayed focused on this goal for over three years.

Focusing on my strong desire to see Gina in our home allowed my 3–di-mensional sales skills to shine. As I made the transition back into the entertainment industry, I took an entry–level position at a video duplica-tion company. In my new position, I developed a sales department, wrote the company's sales manual, and trained the sales and leadership teams. Within eighteen months, I had received three promotions, including the promotion to vice president of the company. My desires were being turned into realities as I started to earn a commission on every sale generated by the company.

My desire for owning our home empowered me far more than what a mere paycheck could do. Times may have been tough, but I focused on that home until our realtor handed us the keys! My desire allowed me to drive my sales vehicle directly to my goal.

A sales professional without desire is like an engine without fuel. Even the best vehicle will fail to perform, when it is lacking the necessary fuel. An idle engine creates no movement. Your sales efforts need momentum, not only to get things started, but to keep things moving. A deeper desire yields a more powerful fuel.

DEVELOP YOUR DESIRE

Everyone enters the sales profession with a common objective: to earn money. No one sells for free. At least they do not do it for free for long. If you do not make money, your sales career will be short–lived. Regardless of how good your product is or how unique your service is, you must sell them to survive.

When I started in sales, I desired to make money. I needed to put food on the table, keep the lights on, and make sure that my wife was not dealing with financial stress on top of her cancer treatments. I was excited about making money, but I discovered that my desires were much deeper than my commission checks.

I know that you want to make more money, but do you have strong de-sires? Do you have a goal that is strong enough to move you to action, no matter what circumstances you face? Too many people limit their ability to grow by shrinking the scope of their desires. I often ask sales associ-ates what their main desire is and they almost unanimously say, "To make more money."

Non–dimensional salespeople are ineffective at helping their clients with their desires because they rarely focus on their own. 3–Dimensional Sales Leaders are guided by strong desires, not dollars. Your desire will define you and will dictate the direction of your career. Some desires become so strong that they help to define your greater purpose – your reason for being here. Are you sellin' for a paycheck or sellin' for a purpose?

3–Dimensional Sales Leaders accomplish their goals because they are able to consistently tap into what moves them – their strongest desires. If your desires are weak, you will have a better chance of winning the lottery than succeeding in sales.

YOUR DESIRES BECOME YOUR GOALS

Too often, people set out to accomplish their sales goals, and that's it. They break out a pad and pen and write down items they wish to accomplish. Most get off to a strong start, but soon lose momentum and allow their sales goals to fade, yet many of these unaccomplished sales goals could have had a significant impact in their lives.

Salespeople give up on sales goals because they lack the proper perception about goals. I accomplish goals because I view them as pieces of the puzzle to my *Big Picture*. With that in mind, developing your *Big Picture* will not only help you to set and accomplish your sales goals, it will help you to accomplish any goal. Every goal you set is a necessary piece of an important puzzle; one that will help you to experience a greater life when you connect the pieces. Connecting your goals will allow you to gain a complete picture of the life you desire and deserve.

We all share some common desires: freedom, security, time, and peace of mind. To start your transformation into a 3–Dimensional Sales Leader, identify the three greatest desires in your life. For example: put my child through college, become debt free, start my own business, contribute more time to charity. Next, list three sales goals that will help you to achieve those desires. For example: develop ten more prospects per week, set five additional appointments per week, recruit two new team members, increase sales volume by 25%.

My 3 Strongest Desires:

1. _____

2. _____

3. _____

3 Sales Goals that will help me to achieve my Desires:

1. _____

2. _____

3. _____

When you focus on strong *Desires*, you will be empowered with an unwavering *Determination*!

CHAPTER 2

DETERMINATION

...must be stronger than your challenges.

I made the choice to pursue a career in sales out of desperation, not preparation. When Gina was diagnosed with cancer, time was of the essence. The time I needed to dedicate to being her caregiver was eaten up by my commute, and my dollars were guzzled away by my gas tank. The opportunity to earn money and control my schedule was limited. As I narrowed my options, I realized that a sales job would best suit our circumstances.

At this time, success was not on my mind; only survival. Without a nest egg to fall back on, I needed to earn money. I not only wanted my sales career to work, I needed it to work! My desire was strong, but it would be my determination that would help me make it through the challenging times that Gina and I experienced.

I may not have had a background in sales, or experience in the financial services industry, but my livelihood was now 100% based on my ability to sell financial products on commission. If I failed to close business, we did not eat. And when I say 'we', I mean my wife with cancer and my two sons with appetites! Yes, I had a strong desire to provide for my family, but it would take more than that to stay on course.

Selling seemed tough and my circumstances seemed even tougher. It reminded me of the day I stepped off of the bus at the Marine Corps Recruiting Depot. It was in the summer of 1987 and I was eighteen years old. My desire to become a U.S. Marine was strong, but it would be my determination to make it out of boot camp, despite the rigors of recruit training, that would keep me going.

The young men in my platoon had the desire to become Marines, but some lacked the determination to complete the three phases of boot camp. Not every recruit graduated as a U.S. Marine, even though each of us had a strong desire to wear our dress blues. Possessing an unwavering determination will keep you on the path to your desires.

Many salespeople have the desire to become more successful, but not everyone has the determination to see it through. Desire gets you moving, but determination keeps you going. My circumstances were not optimum for beginning a career in sales. Perhaps yours are not either. But being determined makes the difference.

IS SELLING TOUGH?

The sales profession is one of the most lucrative career opportunities in today's business world. But almost every salesperson, regardless of their level of success, has the perception that *selling is tough*. I have heard it a thousand times, and I will probably hear it a thousand more, because there is an ounce of truth to this statement. After all, if selling was easy, everyone would do it eagerly.

Every solid achievement carries with it a price. Serving our country is one of my greatest personal accomplishments. I would not change a thing, not even the extreme physical and mental challenges I endured to earn the title of U.S. Marine. Our training was tough and no one would say otherwise. But I attribute those difficulties to becoming a better Marine.

Becoming a 3–Dimensional Sales Leader has been one of the most rewarding experiences in my life. But it, too, came at a price. It was challenging, frustrating, stressful. Look, it was tough! I am sure that you can relate. But it will be your ability to make it through the tough times that will make you a more effective salesperson. Your determination is your secret weapon.

Selling is simple, but many salespeople fail because their level of determination is weaker than their challenges. Even with a strong desire, salespeople face numerous obstacles which prevent them from staying consistent with the basic steps of selling. Think of it as walking a straight line. Most of us are capable of walking a straight line, but what happens when we try to do it on a small boat? And what happens when that boat is tossed back and forth by waves? Although the line remains the same, it becomes much more difficult to walk it when the circumstances change. A simple walk just got tough!

Too many salespeople jump overboard as soon as their sales 'boat' begins to rock a little. A powerful determination will help you overcome any waves in your path. While selling may not always be a walk in the park, it is a simple process. Most great accomplishments require basic steps to be taken, by determined individuals. Successfully selling is no different.

Selling can be as simple as losing weight. Please note that I did not say it is as easy as losing weight! Millions of people desire to be in better shape, but not everyone is determined to do what is required. Losing weight is a simple process: consistently eat right and exercise. Selling is a simple process: consistently contact people and complete more sales. Is there more to both, minimizing your weight and maximizing your sales? Yes, but the basic components are never complicated. Only the circumstances of selling become complicated.

TOUGHEN UP YOUR PERCEPTION

One of the best ways to create an unwavering determination is to toughen up your attitude toward sales. Let's talk about how tough selling really is. The perception that selling is tough is just that, a perception. And perceptions can be changed. I was so determined to sell that I focused on changing my own meaning of what *tough* really meant.

When I first started my career in sales, I probably would have agreed that selling is tough, and my small commission checks proved that point. Now, I am more certain than ever that selling is not tough. Selling is 'T.U.F.'

and 3-Dimensional Sales Leaders need to be T.U.F. in order to experience greater results.

Being **T.U.F.** allows your clients to:

T – Trust you

U – Understand you

F – Follow you

Becoming 3-dimensional is about building these three aspects with your clients. If you only achieve one or two, you may lose your clients to someone who can target all of them. Be determined to achieve all three!

When a client trusts and understands you, they will probably buy from you, at least initially. But if a client also follows you, to their goals, they will remain with you, refer more clients to you, and help you to hit your goals. That is my perception of tough sales and it serves me well. Does your perception about tough sales serve you? If not, perhaps you should change it.

A weak perception is strong enough to damage your sales efforts. Remember, increasing your sales results is about changing your perception of sales. It does not matter how great your product is, how valuable your service is, or how fine-tuned your sales skills are. If you are not determined to be T.U.F., you will be unable to influence people to consistently buy from you.

I was determined to do more than just complete sales; I was determined to open more opportunities! Succeeding in sales takes a great deal of hard work and determination. Do not be afraid to get your hands dirty. My camouflage uniform was rarely clean during basic training, but the positive effects of boot camp will continue to stay with me throughout my life!

Although your goals may be powerful, I know that you will encounter some tough times while on your journey to accomplish them. Possessing a strong determination will allow you to push back when life pushes you.

I define a successful sales career as, 'a simple process, with multiple layers of difficulty, consistently performed by a determined leader with strong desires.' Does this definition work you? I have always possessed a strong desire that has helped me through tough times. My determination not only got me back on my feet, but kept me motivated and in pursuit of my goals.

I am sure that you have experienced difficult times during your sales journey. We have all faced seemingly insurmountable obstacles, but we only lose when we give up. If you continue to sell, tough times are inevitable. Such difficulties do not last, but determined 3–Dimensional Sales Leaders do. Your unwavering determination will help you to stay on track to accomplish any sales goal.

> *"Let me tell you the secret that has led me to my*
> *goal: my strength lies solely in my tenacity."*
>
> ~ *Louis Pasteur*

My experience in the Marine Corps and the entertainment industry may not have prepared me for selling. But I am writing a book about dramatically improving your sales results, because I dramatically improved mine. I refused to give up! When I made a commitment to achieve my desires, my first task focused on improving my perception of sales.

When you exhibit an unwavering **Determination**, you will make more meaningful **Decisions**!

Chapter 3

Decisions

...must be focused on serving.

Today, what is the single most important decision that will be made to ensure your success? That sounds like a loaded question, but the answer means the difference between selling and failing, earning and yearning, winning and losing. The answer is the combined result of all other decisions made in your business. The answer is simple: the most important decision will be made by your client; it is their decision to buy from you!

In sales, the choices you make are like the wooden slats of a bridge, spanning across an abyss. Each smart decision you make builds a section to your bridge; each careless one damages a section. Building a sturdy platform of wise decisions will allow your client to confidently step across the bridge of *choices and decisions*, and choose you on the other side. Some clients may only take one or two steps before choosing to buy from you, while others may travel the entire length of the bridge to arrive at that decision.

Developing new clients and maintaining existing ones is a never–ending journey. If you are not consciously selling people about what you bring to the table, then you are subconsciously selling them about what your competition brings to the table! It is your choice, but your clients will make the final decision. Your job is to influence their buying process and the only way you can do that is by making smart decisions.

"Sometimes it's the smallest decisions that can change your life forever."
~ Keri Russell

Early in my sales career, I focused my attention on choosing the right products and services, those that best served my clients' *needs*. As I became more dimensional in my sales approach, I focused my attention on making the right decisions, those that best served my clients' *goals*.

The choices you make, both big and small, should never be taken lightly. Your decisions enable your clients to trust you, understand you, and follow you (T.U.F.). Every day, everything you choose to do will impact someone's decision to buy from you, refer people to you, and stay with you.

What if a client does not choose you? Even the most seasoned sales professionals mistake their client's decision not to buy from them as something they did wrong. While there may be some truth to that, I perceive it as their choice to buy from someone else. That empowers me to work harder to influence their decisions.

THE PSYCHOLOGY OF BUYING

The choices you make ultimately impact the buyer's final answer. Although there are many outside factors that help buyers to finalize their decisions, the decisions that you make will always be a key factor.

3–Dimensional Sales Leaders experience greater results because they can more easily recognize what constitutes a client's decision–making process. They are better prepared to help clients to accomplish their goals.

Here are some of the reasons that people base their final purchase decision on:

- Solve problems
- Avoid pain
- Impress others
- Make money
- Experience pleasure
- Be popular
- Increase security
- Gain comfort
- Eliminate criticism
- Save money

While there are others, you will find that your clients' decisions to buy fall somewhere within these criteria. It is your job to find out which reason, or combination of reasons, influences their choices. Too many salespeople focus only on what their clients need. Make the choice to identify *why* they need something and you will more easily sell *what* they need.

Your clients have desires too. If their *desires* are strong enough, they will be *determined* to achieve them by making the *decision* to buy the necessary products and services. Regardless of what is purchased, people are ultimately making their choice to buy from you based on the decisions you have made.

Your client typically knows why they select you or select someone else. As they reach their final decision, many of their objections may remain unspoken. While people are never obligated to share those with you, 3–Dimensional Sales Leaders are able to peel off the layers to uncover the client's decision–making process.

My clients perceive me as a 3–Dimensional Sales Leader focused on making the choices that will help them to accomplish their goals. How do your clients perceive you? Nothing affects someone's perception of you more than the decisions you make.

MAKE THE DECISION TO BUILD RELATIONSHIPS

Your ability to understand and influence buying decisions of a client will largely rest on your relationship with that individual. Is your relationship with your client stronger than your competitor's relationship with them? Strong relationships overcome strong objections! I have found that the deeper the relationship I have with the client, the less influencing I need to do.

To assess my decision–making skills, I typically rate my relationship with my clients. I use a simple scale of '1' to '5', with '5' being best. Early in my career, I made the valuable decision to use high standards. In fact, I rarely assign a '5'. When my client is a '4' or lower, I still have work to do! Rate your client relationships on a scale of '1' to '5' and invest the necessary time to upgrade their rating.

Many inexperienced salespeople rate their relationships much higher than they should. By setting your relationship rating lower, you will make more effort to influence their decisions. I have only given a few clients a rating of '5': my mom, my wife, other family members, and very close friends. It takes time to develop a relationship that is so strong that it requires little to no influence. My '5's trust me, understand me, and follow me to their goals. There is no salesperson who could ever sell a product to my '5's as long as I offered it, too! Are your clients that loyal to you? Do you want them to be?

We rarely sell exclusive, one–of–a–kind items. Most products and services can be purchased from another salesperson, or bought online. Most people are not looking for a new salesperson, but everyone prefers a 3–Dimensional Sales Leader who makes decisions aligned with their goals.

This relationship–rating works both ways! If your clients were to rate their relationship with you, what rating would you deserve?

THE PSYCHOLOGY OF SELLING

For salespeople, each day starts with the opportunity to make critical choices; choices that will help to achieve their sales results. Consistently making smart decisions is paramount and one of the greatest choices you will make in your sales career is adding depth to your sales efforts. Become a 3–Dimensional Sales Leader to bring more value to the lives of your clients and positively influence their decision–making process.

Every day we make choices, big and small, that have the potential to impact that one key decision we are all striving for: that people buy from us. We decide what time we will wake up and what attitude will guide us through the day. We select whom we will call, what we will say, and when we will schedule appointments. We make the all–important decision to invest our time or waste it. We choose whether to succeed or to fail. The decision is ours.

Most salespeople do not intend to fail, but along the way, many end up making the wrong decisions. Our choices are influenced by what we focus on. Those who operate in a reactive mode make poor decisions based on their circumstances. Such choices will have long-lasting, negative effects on their sales careers.

Non-dimensional sales decisions are based on:

- Fear – Fear of rejection
- Worry – Worrying about not making enough money
- Reactions – Misreading someone's body language and responses
- Assumptions – Assuming what people are thinking or wanting
- Comfort – Staying in a comfort zone of mediocrity

These factors are detrimental to sales and lead salespeople to make the wrong decisions.

3-Dimensional Sales Leaders continue to strengthen their bridges by operating in a proactive mode, making decisions based on the desires of their clients. These choices will have long-lasting, positive effects on their sales careers.

3-dimensional sales decisions are based on:

- Identifying goals
- Gathering information
- Conducting research
- Presenting solutions
- Understanding objections

Identifying Goals – Remember, your clients' goals are always far more important than any product or service. Those who pay particular attention to accomplishing these goals are more likely to accomplish their own. Making choices that bring your clients closer to their goals will often result in decisions that bring you closer to a sale.

Gathering Information – Making the decision to ask the right questions allows you to gather the information necessary to truly take care of your clients.

Conducting Research – Making the choice to do your due diligence and uncover opportunities that will benefit your client will separate you from your competition.

Presenting Solutions – Many salespeople misuse the time with clients to present the reasons the client should select their products and services. Make the decision to focus on presenting viable solutions to your clients, and you will develop lasting relationships and repeat business.

Understanding Objections – Far too many salespeople view objections as a sign that the client does not want to buy. Objections signal a lack of understanding. Choose to perceive objections as opportunities to provide clarity and you will build more trust.

To elevate your results, move from reactive decision–making to proactive decision–making. Everything is your choice! I have seen far too many salespeople fail to complete a sale that they considered 'in the bag', because they did not make all of the right choices involved in influencing their clients. Nothing is in the bag until the client *decides* it is!

MAKE THE DECISION TO SERVE

What is the best decision you can make today? The decision that will improve your sales results is to serve your clients, not just sell to them. Serving your clients will literally separate you from your competition. How do you want your clients to perceive you? As someone who *sells* them or someone who *serves* them?

Most potential buyers know someone selling the same thing that you sell. It may be an acquaintance, a close friend, or even a family member. I have met with clients who have had all three, and I have successfully been the person they chose to do business with. It can be tough to beat out a strong personal relationship, but ultimately, most people will choose the person who serves them best.

Serving your clients means that you are making the decision to put their needs above yours. It is a commitment to make their goals your priority. That sounds like common sense, but not all salespeople put their clients first. Many feel deserving of the sale just because they made a presentation, did some research, or provided a proposal.

I have never seen a person quit their sales career because they were experiencing great results. But I have seen them give up because they could not make it beyond their challenges. By focusing on adding depth to your sales efforts, you are enhancing your perception of selling and your clients' perception of buying.

A 3-DIMENSIONAL VIEW

To fully become a 3–Dimensional Sales Leader, focus on your desires, rely on your determination, and make the best decisions. Keep your 3–D glasses on at all times, and you will view all components of the sales process in a new light, significantly enhancing your performance and drastically increasing your results.

Just like you, I encountered a lot of obstacles on my sales journey. There is no greater way to navigate around those obstacles than to have a 3–dimensional perspective. It continues to work for me, and I am confident that it will work for you!

Now it is time to discover the essential sales gears that will allow you to keep your sales machine humming!

PART II

KEEP YOUR SALES GEARS TURNING

PART II

KEEP YOUR SALES GEARS TURNING

The heart of your sales machine.

We live in a world that relies predominantly on machines – for everything! Most people and businesses would not know how to function without the devices that surround them. We count on machines for virtually every area in our lives: computers to coffee makers, automobiles to televisions, and cell phones to air conditioners. If we fail to properly maintain them, they will break down and can dramatically affect our quality of life – especially the coffee maker!

In sales, machines allow us to communicate with our clients, perform research, and process business. We drive to appointments, fly to business conferences, send price quotes via e–mail, receive timely information through faxes, and utilize customized software programs to be more efficient in our day–to–day operations. And those represent only a small percentage of the machines we use each day.

Though important, the machines we use in our business are nothing compared to the *sales machine* of our business. Your sales machine is the system you use for marketing, the development of a client base and the successful movement of products and services. Every day, your highest priority should be to create new relationships and build existing ones. Successfully systematizing this process will have a dramatic impact on your career.

Although there are hundreds of presentation styles, selling strategies, and closing techniques that can help to improve sales results, there are five basic gears that allow your sales machine to operate predictably and prof-itably.

The 5 Gears of Your Sales Machine:

- Gear 1: Prospecting
- Gear 2: Contacting
- Gear 3: Presenting
- Gear 4: Set–Up
- Gear 5: Follow–Up

Powered by your desires, determination, and decisions, these five gears, when operating in unison, will enable you to consistently develop new clients, sell more products, earn referrals, and maintain existing business – regardless of what industry you are in. To experience new levels of success, it is your responsibility to keep the gears of your sales machine constantly turning, effectively and efficiently.

People try to achieve consistent sales results without consistently following a system. Salespeople who attempt to run a successful operation without using a marketing system are like athletes who try to get in shape without a regimented workout routine. Even great athletes cannot expect to see results just by showing up at the gym. It is their performance at the gym that produces results.

Selling is no different. Showing up in your office means nothing, if you are not running a sales machine for marketing. Too many salespeople take a reactive approach to marketing, waiting patiently for the next lead to fall into their lap. Remember, that which easily falls into your lap can just as easily bounce right out!

When you turn on your sales machine, you become pro–active. By keeping your gears turning, you will increase your ability to expand your client base exponentially. The only thing you will wait for is your commission checks to hit! An effective sales machine is the key to success for any business, team, or individual sales associate to achieve greater results.

Your sales machine is an agenda of repetitious activities that allows you to effectively market yourself and your products, by focusing on building and growing relationships with your clients.

RELATIONSHIP MARKETING

I have sold for companies that provided leads and sold for companies that did not. I have gathered leads from e-mail inquiries, incoming phone calls, post cards, and networking events. As I assessed my results, I realized that the best way to increase my sales was to focus on Relationship Marketing.

Relationship Marketing is the sales technique used by 3-Dimensional Sales Leaders, which taps into the word-of-mouth power of their warm market. Whether you are new to sales or have been selling for decades, you have an existing base of contacts that you can expand to develop new clients, sell more products, and open up new opportunities. The more people who know what you sell, the more people they can tell!

While selling financial services and media solutions, I trained individuals and teams, and taught them to do the same. As a sales coach, I have also worked with people in a wide array of other, unrelated fields such as construction, legal services, tax-planning, health and fitness, jewelry and clothing.

Although each industry requires specialized product knowledge, successful sales results can always be narrowed down to your ability to turn the five basic gears of sales. The biggest mistake I encounter is allowing one of your gears to stop! How well your sales machine performs is up to you. Do you want yours to be held together with duct tape and chewing gum, or do you want it to be well-oiled and fine-tuned?

I have often coached sales professionals who believed that they had no one to target. They say things like, "I don't have a warm market." Or, "I have already gone through my list." Or even, "I don't know anyone." A salesperson who does not 'know anyone' is out of business! By teaching people how to fire up their sales machine, I have seen them create extensive and powerful new contacts.

There are nearly seven billion people in our world. Someone needs what you have. By keeping your gears turning, you will uncover many new prospects and develop more clients than you ever thought possible. It is up to you to crank up the power of your sales machine and reach those people, before your competition does! Even those who claim to have no list, will multiply their new contacts by ensuring that all five gears remain in motion.

TURN YOUR GEARS

When I sold financial services, I made the mistake of assuming that my clients knew everything I sold. Because they bought one product, I figured they knew the rest of my product line. I remember delivering a life insurance policy to a close friend of mine. As she signed her policy, I discovered that she had just refinanced her house. Although I offered mortgage loans, I did not do this one.

When I reminded her that I was a loan officer, she said, "Oh shoot! I didn't know." She associated me with one product. I had failed to run my sales machine effectively, and it cost me a sale. My commission on the life insurance product was about $200. My commission on the loan would have been over $2,000! That mistake made me realize how important it was to consistently turn each of the gears of my sales machine.

It is easy to miss an easy sale, but it is also unnecessary. Your sales machine ensures that your relationships grow stronger, allowing you to know more about your clients, and your clients to know more about you.

Relationships are built and strengthened by several factors. But the most effective way to build strong, long–term relationships is by having *constant personal communication* – before, during and after the sale! I missed the mortgage sale because I stopped the selling process after the life insurance sale. But my client never stopped the buying process!

Another reason that people miss out on developing strong relationships is because they overlook someone who does not appear to need their product. But often, that same person may know someone else who needs your product. A properly running sales machine will ensure that no one falls through the cracks, even the people you do not yet know. A strong relationship helps you to expand your client base – without you asking for their help!

Your sales machine is organized so you can reap the rewards of Relationship Marketing.

The Benefits of Your Sales Machine:

- Improve client retention
- Open up new sales possibilities from existing clients
- Increase referrals
- Increase production

You cannot expect to successfully develop new clients, properly maintain existing ones, and consistently sell new products unless you have a proven system. But, 3–Dimensional Sales Leaders succeed because they strive to add the human element to a mechanized system.

START YOUR ENGINES!

Losing a client can typically be tracked back to one of your sales gears – usually the one that has stopped turning. Did you prospect them too late? Did you fail to contact them soon enough? Did you skip your presentation? Did you set up their account/new order incorrectly? Of course, it could not be a lack of follow–up, could it?

If any one of your gears is not working, it is a sure sign that your potential client will choose someone who keeps their sales machine operational. Clients want to work with someone who can systematically help them achieve their results. Remember, their goals are on the line. You owe it to them and to yourself to run a sales machine that does not wear out, break down, or stop moving.

By paying close attention to each gear of your sales machine, you will be able to increase your effectiveness. As your sales skills increase, the size of your gears will grow, allowing your sales machine to run a larger, more profitable business. The larger your gears, the greater your potential. Your personal commitment to these five gears will determine your success!

Consistency is the key to running your sales machine!

CHAPTER 4

GEAR 1 – PROSPECTING

The art of deciding whom to contact.

How much of an impact do you want to have with your sales machine? Are you looking to just scratch the surface of selling? Or do you have the desire to build a thriving, profitable career that also helps others to accomplish their goals? By reading this book, and transforming  yourself into a 3–Dimensional Sales Leader, I think it is safe to say that you are a looking to create a sales machine that will produce new levels of success!

People are easily intimidated and feel uneasy or awkward about the selling process. Selling is a lot like fishing. There are millions of fish in the sea, all willing to bite, but it will be the fisherman with the best system that will consistently bring in the biggest haul.

Fishing is much more than just casting your bait into the water. Successful fishermen do not wait for a hit, they plan for a catch. Like selling, it involves a great deal of prospecting. Deciding which fish to go after is a start, but there is more. What is the best time of day to fish? Which location will produce the best results? What type of bait will work best? What strategies and techniques will you use? Well, the list can go on, and that's just to catch fish. You're trying to catch sales!

Fishing is a sport, with winners and losers. You can be a competitive fisherman or treat it as a relaxing hobby. Some people fish as a form of relaxation and are not bothered, if they do not catch anything. But unlike fishing, there is nothing relaxing about letting a sale get away. Do you know any salespeople who treat their career as a hobby, just sitting in the boat and hoping they get a bite?

Anyone can hold a fishing rod and think they're a fisherman. In sales, anyone can hold a sales position and think they are a salesperson. It happens all too often. Here is an important fact about successful salespeople – they sell. Here is an important fact about selling wisely – it starts with effective prospecting.

Prospecting is not just an action you take; it is the art of choosing whom to contact. It is one of the most important decisions you will make each day. Like a champion fisherman, a 3–Dimensional Sales Leader invests the necessary time and dedication to prospecting.

Too many salespeople dive right into their contacting efforts but fail to achieve their desired results. Most work hard at turning their Contacting Gear, but put little thought into their Prospecting Gear. If your Prospecting Gear remains idle, you will have less success when turning your Contacting Gear.

Prospecting is much more than mindlessly dumping your phone book onto a piece of paper. Your Prospecting Gear enables the ongoing, detailed identification and analysis of people to contact: the 'who', the 'why', the 'when', and the 'how'. Anyone can make a list of names, but very few can turn names into satisfied clients.

Although I speak and write books for a living, I'm in sales. Each day, I reach out to more people. Contacting them is the only way that I can guarantee to increase my sales results. How would you like to be able to guarantee that your sales results constantly improve? Your ability to effectively contact people and influence them to buy starts with your decision to turn your Prospecting Gear.

THE POWER OF A PROSPECTING LIST

The best part about a successful sales career is that you do not have to contact everyone in order to generate sales, but you must contact someone. Perhaps your products and services can be offered to a large customer base. That's great, but you cannot contact all of them in one day. Planning your contacting, by properly prospecting, will increase your chances for greater results.

What is a prospecting list? My prospecting list is an ever–growing list of my warm contacts who will benefit from my products and services. In turn, they will also introduce me to their warm contacts, who will also benefit from my products and services. My prospecting list is endless, but highly prioritized. How you work your prospecting list determines how well you make contact.

I keep my Prospecting Gear turning every day. For me, it started with making a list of people I knew and rating the strengths of my relationship with them from '1' to '5'. Your list is important for many reasons, but none more crucial than to help accomplish your goals. Remember, the first step is to identify important goals and then write them down. Many salespeople view their prospecting list as a list of buyers, but I perceive it as a list of people with goals. My objective is to transform each prospect into a client, and each client into more prospects.

I am very focused on growing my list, to the extent that I track how many names I add to it each day. If you are operating as a 3–Dimensional Sales Leader, you will add new names on a daily basis. Always focus on expanding your prospecting list.

STARTING YOUR PROSPECTING LIST

When I began my sales career in the financial services industry, I was excited to contact people and make sales. Before I picked up the phone, my trainer instructed me to make a list of everyone I knew. I just wanted to get on the phone, but alright, I would do a list. I quickly broke out my pen and was ready to fill up the sheet with names. But only twelve names trickled out of my pen and onto my list. I thought I knew more people than that.

I soon realized that I was limiting my ability to develop my list because I was focusing only on the people I thought I could sell. A great prospecting list is about more than selling, it is about reaching. In re-evaluating the true purpose of my list, I was able to identify everyone I knew. I focused on five specific categories to build my list, and it quickly grew from twelve to more than 250 names! As you start your list, or rebuild your existing one, focus on five key categories.

The 5 Prospecting Categories:

1. Family members
2. Friends
3. Co-workers/former co-workers
4. Classmates – high school/college
5. Professionals

Think big! List every family member you can. Even your cousins have cousins, who are not your cousins! The same holds true for friends. Your friends have friends, who are not your friends, yet!

The category of professionals should include your insurance agents, realtors, loan officers, dentists, doctors, pastors, personal trainers, etc. Think about the warm contacts they have. If only they knew what you sold, perhaps they could refer you to someone in their warm market (your cold market).

How many names are racing through your head right now? Start jotting them down on a piece of paper. At the end of this chapter, you will have a template to create your own 3-D Prospecting List.

You never run out of people to contact when you know how to turn your Prospecting Gear!

EXPANDING YOUR PROSPECTING LIST

A prospecting list is never complete. It starts with your warm contacts – people you have a relationship with. So it is safe to say that the only way you can expand your list is by adding new names – people you do not have a relationship with. But how can you add the names of people you do not yet know? You enlist the support of the people you know. They will melt down the barrier between your warm market and the cold market.

I do not operate in the cold market, and will not participate in calling and knocking on the doors of people I have no relationship with. That does not motivate me at all. My efforts are devoted to getting the word out to my warm market. Understanding that there are far more people whom I do not know than people I do know, I encourage my warm market to introduce me to their warm market.

I use the five gears of my sales machine to develop and grow my prospecting list: I add names to my list as I contact people (Gear 2), make presentations (Gear 3), set up their accounts/orders (Gear 4), and follow–up with them (Gear 5).

When a client feels that you are only interested in a sale, they may be hesitant to help expand your list. However, most people will gladly introduce you to their warm market, when they feel that you focus on their best interests.

Let's say your prospecting list is 100 people strong. Although that's a great list, it pales in comparison to the number of people still out there whom you do not know. I believe that each person on your prospecting list can easily make a list of ten people you need to know. That means that you are one step closer to warmly meeting an additional 1,000 new people. If you could develop relationships with those 1,000, each of the ten people they know would turn into an additional 10,000 names! You should never run out of people to contact.

People who feel that they have no one to contact do not understand the power of their Prospecting Gear. When it comes to experiencing greater sales results, I always have an outcome for placing people on my list. Often, my outcome is to be introduced to people I do not know. I rarely prospect just to make a sale. I always prospect to expand my warm market list.

By successfully operating your sales machine, your warm market will literally 'break the ice' with the cold market and exponentially expand your prospecting list.

HAVE AN OUTCOME FOR YOUR PROSPECTING LIST

How many people do you want to sell to? The correct answer is all of them. While we know that is virtually impossible to do, you can increase your chances when you have an outcome for creating your list. Prospecting is much more than closing your eyes, putting your finger on your list, and guessing whom you will contact. When performed with an outcome, prospecting allows you to control your contacting and increases your chances of selling.

Salespeople perceive the process of prospecting differently, but they all have one thing in common. They ask a very important question; a question that reveals their outcome – their reason for generating the prospecting list in the first place.

The 3 Prospecting Questions:

1. Whom can I call?
2. Whom can I sell?
3. Whom can I help?

WHOM CAN I CALL? Some salespeople call their prospects but fail to ask for the sale. They call to get through their daily phone calls. It is an awkward call because they never get to the real reason of why they were calling.

WHOM CAN I SELL? Some salespeople call their prospects but only ask for the sale. Many prospects will start to avoid calls from people who offer nothing more than the opportunity to buy from them.

WHOM CAN I HELP? 3–Dimensional Sales Leaders call because they are prepared to help their prospects to accomplish their goals. By focusing on an outcome like this, your prospects will be more likely to help you expand your list with referrals.

Look at the names on your list and think about the question that enters your mind regarding each person. Whom can I call? Whom can I sell? Whom can I help? Your prospecting list is a work in progress – it is never complete. If your list stops growing, your business stops growing! On the next page, use the simple 3–D Prospecting List template to create your own dynamic list of prospects.

NAME: List your prospect's name.

RATING: Rate your relationship with your prospect, '5' being best.

OUTCOME: Why are they on this list? Remember the three
                      prospecting questions.

DATE: The date you put them on this list. Do not let too much
                      time go by before you contact them.

> ### A Leader's
> ### Perspective
> Focus most of your thoughts on the 'Outcome' column.

The 3–D Prospecting List holds 25 names, so you may need three or four sheets to list your growing warm market. Perhaps you will need more than that!

Yes, you can contact someone without prospecting, but why would you?

3–D PROSPECTING LIST

NAME	RATING	OUTCOME	DATE

YOUR PROSPECTING GEAR IS TURNING

The final step of prospecting is to decide whom you will contact and in which order. As you look over your prospecting list, think beyond mere sales. Focus on what you have to offer and how you can add value to their lives.

Think about the most important prospecting question you can ask yourself: "Whom can I help?" Regardless if you are new to sales or a seasoned professional, examine your prospecting list with your 3–D glasses on. Remember, your *Desire*, your *Determination*, and your *Decisions* will power your sales machine and keep all of your sales gears turning.

I typically contact everyone on my list, but I cannot do it successfully by using the rapid–fire method of calling – just calling to say that I called. I prefer the laser–focused method – concentrating on ten prospects to contact per day. In a short time period, you will achieve more by properly contacting just ten people per day, rather than speeding through 25 calls each day.

The 3 Criteria of Successful Prospecting:

1. How can I build my relationship?
2. What do they need from me?
3. Whom do they know?

Based on these three questions, everyone can be contacted. Too often, I see salespeople disqualify a prospect too hastily, but when you only focus on sales, your prospect may not qualify. However, they may qualify to be contacted by your competition. Make it a habit to contact everyone on your list. Otherwise, why are they on it?

I qualify at least ten prospects the night before contacting anyone. I use this time to analyze my existing relationship with each person and identify ways that I can elevate it. I focus on areas where I can help them. And I think of any referrals they may have for me.

If they own a business, I make sure to learn more about their industry and the products that might be beneficial to their company. The internet is an effective tool to educate yourself about your potential client's business.

Prospecting is not a numbers game. Instead, it is the art of deciding whom to contact.

Prospecting enhances **Contacting!**

CHAPTER 5

GEAR 2 – CONTACTING

The mastery of setting the next appointment.

I love it when I answer the phone and a person on the other end says, "I want to buy something right now and I want to buy it from you!" Don't you love it when that happens? But how often does that occur in your business? I have done the math and come to discover that it  does not happen enough to make a living. Most prospects do not initiate the contact. Even the best laid–out prospecting list will not make the calls for you. That's why it is our responsibility to consistently turn our Contacting Gear.

Remember, sales is a leadership position. And what is the number one quality of an effective leader? It is their ability to effectively and efficiently communicate. Although there are many ways to communicate with your prospects, you must consistently get across the same basic message: that it is in their best interest to choose you.

Many salespeople can develop lists, with dozens, if not hundreds of prospects. But the idea of contacting those people intimidates them and understandably so. A lot is riding on that first call. Everyone wants to make contact the right way, but the fear of doing it the wrong way can be a major hurdle to overcome. Even though my prospecting list was powerful, I was hesitant to pick up that phone. Understanding why you are contacting someone allows you to overcome that fear. The goal of contacting is to set up the next appointment!

Contacting is like feeding pigeons at the park. I once saw a young child, his hands filled with popcorn, run toward a flock of birds on the grass. There must have been nearly a hundred pigeons looking to be fed. The idea of feeding them put a big smile across the boy's face. As he neared the birds, he screamed with excitement and threw his popcorn in the air. He certainly made 'contact' with the pigeons. He let them know he was there and had something great to offer them. But despite their hunger, they flew off, without eating any of the popcorn.

The boy's grandfather watched his face turn from joy to sadness as a few feathers fell back to the ground. He knelt down and helped his grandson pick up the popcorn, then walked him over to a bench. As they sat, he told him to toss a few pieces out. The boy did so, and eventually the birds flew back for the popcorn. They continued this process until all of the pigeons had returned, including a few new ones.

Although his intentions were good, the boy's techniques scared away his prospects. Has this ever happened to you? Have you ever been so excited about what you had to offer that you quickly picked up the phone, punched in a number, and showered your prospect with your 'popcorn'? Although you knew you did a good job on the phone, you could not figure out why that person stopped returning your calls. Your Contacting Gear is meant to do much more than just allow you to speak to someone. It is designed to provide you with the opportunity to make contact with your prospects and set up a face-to-face appointment.

Remember, you are striving to build relationships. Strong relationships are built in person, face-to-face. I can tell my wife that I love her over the phone, but it has much more meaning when I say it in person. The true purpose of contacting is to get you in position to transform your prospect into a client and to encourage your clients to trust you with referrals.

You contact your warm market to set appointments. What is the best method of contacting? Any form of contacting that leads to an appointment is a useful form of contacting. If you are able to send smoke signals and achieve great results, then keep sending those smoke signals. In order to set face–to–face appointments, I have used every form of contacting, but three ways work best for me.

1. E–mail
2. Phone call
3. Drop–by

While each method can help you to set an appointment, it may take a combination of all three to accomplish that objective.

CONTACTING IS NOT...

In addition to personally making contact with thousands of prospects, I have observed the contacting efforts of countless sales professionals. While most salespeople make calls with the best of intentions, filled with certainty and passion, they rarely achieve the results they were hoping for. Regardless of what industry people sell in, I have found a common mistake made by most sales professionals – they say too much during the initial contact.

Many salespeople keep a prospect on the phone for five, ten, fifteen, and even thirty minutes as they pitch their products. I have seen them easily get side–tracked and discuss things unrelated to what they sell.

Some of your prospects are polite and do not share their true thoughts: "I want off of this phone call." Think about it from their perspective. If you talk this long on the phone, how long are you going to talk in person? The more you talk, the less likely you are to set an appointment. Contacting is not a presentation – that falls under Gear 3! Say enough to peak their interest and leave the rest for your presentation.

By eliminating your lengthy 'state of the union' speeches, you will have more valuable time to make laser–focused contacting. Are there times when a prospect will want to stay on the phone and chat? Yes, but it is your responsibility to keep your Contacting Gear turning, set an appointment, then contact your next prospect. Because most of my calls are made to get face-to-face time with my clients, I tend to limit the amount of time I am on the phone to two minutes or less.

I have read e-mails that were so lengthy, I felt like I was reading a book. I do the same thing with long e-mails that your prospects do – I delete them! I have also seen a quick drop-by almost turn into a sleep over. Have you ever had a guest stay too long at your house? It is called 'overstaying your welcome'. When you do that to a prospect, you will not get invited back for an actual appointment, nor will you receive referrals.

Whether you use e-mails, phone calls, or drop-bys, they are best done with as few words as possible. But your words must impress your prospect enough to want to get together. And do not mistake courtesy for consent. Rarely will someone tell you that you are bugging them, even when you are.

Every spoken word has greater meaning in person. Just as 'I love you' goes much further in front of someone than it does over the phone, many salespeople rob themselves of the relationship-building power by failing to get face-to-face.

CONTACTING IS...

Now that we know what not to do during our contacting time, let's talk about what to do in order to achieve the results you deserve. Although you can contact people at any time of the day, all day long, I have found that I achieve the greatest results when I dedicate a specific time of the day to turning my Contacting Gear. This time period is all about me initiating contact and setting new appointments.

E-mails, phone calls, and drop-bys must be performed at the time of day that ensures the best results. Generally, I try to compose contacting e-mails at night, so people read them first thing in the morning. I make phone calls to businesses later in the morning, allowing people to be settled in at work. I make contacting phone calls to individuals at night, allowing people a chance to have dinner and unwind. When I do drop–bys, I schedule them based on the availability of my prospects. Everyone is unique.

Regardless of *how* you contact, *why* you are contacting is paramount. Contact to set an appointment. You might have success from an e–mail, a phone call, or a drop–by. But often, it takes a combination of these. I perceive contacting like this: my e–mail should lead to a phone call, my phone call should lead to a drop–by, and my drop–by should lead to an appointment. If I cannot get face–to–face after this type of contacting, I need to take a closer look at my relationship with my prospect, and how I am communicating.

Contacting is about staying consistent and creating momentum. There is a big difference between your prospecting list and your contacting list. Your prospecting list is a never–ending roster of people to contact. But your contacting list is a detailed agenda of people you will make contact with on a specific day.

I know that I have been driving the point home that contacting is about setting the next appointment, but you will rarely start a conversation by saying, "Hi, it's Erik, we need to meet right now!" That approach seldom works, even though your outcome is to set the appointment. The reason that I focus on the outcome so much is to prevent me from getting off track. There are a million reasons to contact someone, but the outcome of setting the next appointment should always be at the forefront of your thoughts – if you intend to sell and gather referrals.

Below are some of the reasons I have contacted a prospect (e–mail, phone call, or drop–by) which have turned into an appointment:

- To let my prospect know that I am with a new company.
- To let my prospect know that I have new products and services.
- To update an existing client on the status of their order.
- To personally deliver something to my prospect.
- To inquire about future needs.
- To congratulate my prospect on an achievement: awards, industry recognition, etc.
- To invite my prospect to lunch or a coffee break.
- To simply check in and see if my client needs anything.

There are many reasons to contact but only one outcome.

SCRIPTS

Many salespeople hesitate to use scripts, for fear of sounding unnatural or 'scripted'. I couldn't agree more. There is nothing worse than receiving a sales call and painfully listening to that person reading a scripted message. But I believe in using scripts to keep me on track, especially when I am discussing a new product or service. Scripts allow me to hit key points and achieve greater results. They also allow me to stay on schedule and keep my contacting brief.

A great script for me is more of an outline of important aspects – the reason I am setting the appointment. Scripts allow me to rehearse what I want to say. Too many people make contact but leave out crucial information. There is nothing less professional then calling back and saying, "Oh yeah, I forgot to mention..." How do you forget to mention a key point? A script allows me to highlight the necessary bullet points that need to be made during contacting.

For a lot of people, contacting is one of the most challenging components of selling. By developing a great script and practicing your delivery, you will be natural and will achieve greater results.

Now let's talk about adding a new dimension to your e-mails, phone calls and drop-bys.

E-MAILS

Outcome: *to set an appointment*

Electronic correspondence is an amazing tool for contacting. I use it every day. Please note that I said contacting. It is also a great tool for Follow-Up (Gear 5). But never confuse the two. When I contact prospects through e-mail, it is always short, sweet, and to the point. My objective is to set an appointment.

I tend to stay away from blanket e-mails because they communicate a very impersonal message. Personalizing an e-mail makes it more memorable and usually encourages a reply. There is nothing more frustrating than sending out a great e-mail and not getting a response.

E-mails are easy to do because you can put thought into them to convey the appropriate message prior to sending. But the message must be as powerful as if you are delivering it in person. E-mails can be easily misunderstood without visual cues. A prospect can interpret your words the wrong way, so be very careful not to be vague or ambiguous.

When I send out a contacting e-mail, one that is intended to set an appointment, I always let the person know that I will be calling them. I end my e-mails with, "I will call you later today." Or, "I will give you a call on Tuesday." I constantly strive for live communication. If you are afraid to call someone, how will you do on an appointment?

A Leader's Perspective

Use your e-mails to set up your phone calls.

PHONE CALLS

Outcome: *to set an appointment*

Over the past few years, phones have become so technologically advanced that you can do almost anything with them. You can check your e–mails, take pictures, surf the web, play games, and even use the phone as a video camera. But too often, salespeople forget its main function: to contact people. Many salespeople allow anything and everything to divert them from their next phone call.

Sometimes that phone receiver seems to weigh a thousand pounds. So many thoughts race through your head as you dial the number. As the phone rings, you can feel the sweat on your brow and the pit in your stomach. Oh no, what were you supposed to say? Whom were you calling? You quickly look over your list trying to remember the person you just dialed. Then they answer. You fumble around for a second, then realize whom you called as they say, "Hello?" You manage to get out a well–phrased, "Ah, how's it going?"

After a little small talk, you both say, "Goodbye," and hang up. The conversation was not a bad one, except that you never mentioned why you called. Your calendar is still empty. The reason that salespeople have difficulty making calls is twofold: they lack an outcome and they try to make a presentation. That's too much for you to do on a phone call. Keep it simple.

The flip side of that is when a salesperson is so excited to share their product with someone that they quickly pick up the phone and spout off all of the benefits, only to soon realize that the excitement was not equally shared. That's too much for a prospect to handle on a phone call.

If you have difficulty achieving great results on your phone calls, do yourself a favor and condense what is being said. It is difficult for people to truly see how excited you are through the phone. That is why a contacting call is meant to set an appointment. While your call must be filled with energy and enthusiasm, your mouth can never convey what your eyes can.

I know the power of face–to–face appointments, so I am always clear as to why I am calling. For example, to introduce a new product to a client, your conversation might go something like this: "Hi Bob, how are you? Great, I wanted to give you a quick call to let you know about a new product I've been showing to all of my clients. The feedback has been amazing and I wanted to get your opinion on it. You might even know someone who would benefit from it. I'm swamped this week, but I was hoping we could meet sometime next week..."

In that very brief, no–pressure phone call, you accomplish the following:

- Asked how your prospect was doing
- Let him know the call would be quick
- Let him know you have something new
- Let him know that other people are interested in it
- Let him know that you value his opinion
- Hinted at referrals
- Let him know that you were busy
- Led the conversation to an appointment

That phone call takes less than two minutes and increases your chances of a face–to–face appointment, where the real selling is done. Too many salespeople try to make a presentation and complete the sale on the first phone call. That is a 'hard sell' and no one likes that.

Calling people is fun, when you're calling for the right reason.

A Leader's Perspective   Call people exactly the same way you would want to be called.

DROP-BYS

Outcome: *to set an appointment*

You can compose an e-mail in one minute. A phone call can be done in two minutes. But a drop-by will typically require more time. The drive alone could take an hour. But this is the only form of contacting that uses the face-to-face technique.

The drop-by is a method of contacting that is meant to be brief and usually unannounced. Dropping by allows your prospects to know that you are willing to be there for them. It is a great way to quickly drop off brochures, promotional items, or even a box of donuts.

It is not necessary to call your prospect before dropping by. Even if your prospect is not there, you can leave your drop-off material at the front desk for them. It is always a great gesture. If your prospect is there, you must let them know that you were in the area and wanted to stop in for a moment. Fight the urge to present and keep your contacting as contacting. You should be heading out to see another client anyway, so you do not have time to visit.

When I drop by, most of my prospects invite me to stay. I do not stay – I set an appointment. I am not there to make a presentation. I am there to keep my Contacting Gear turning! Always exhibit the utmost professionalism when you drop-by their business or their home. Your drop-bys should always be based on your relationship with your prospect.

A Leader's Perspective

Schedule your drop-bys with the greatest of detail but always be as natural as possible. You should base your visit on how well your relationship is with your contact.

IT IS ALL ABOUT COMMUNICATION

I have heard that the only people that Americans rank lower than salespeople are politicians. And it was by a narrow margin! Do you know why salespeople are ranked so low? One of the biggest reasons is their communication skills. Your contacting skills change peoples' perception. I never make calls 'from the hip'. I put careful thought into my calls, so I can get my desired results. How powerful are your words? They are powerful enough to shape opinions. It is typically the first thing people judge us on. You know the phrase: you don't get a second chance to make a first impression.

Although the little boy in the park was able to rebound and deliver his popcorn, salespeople rarely get that second opportunity. Even though his popcorn did not change, his plan for delivery did. Your Contacting Gear allows you to map much more than whom you will call, it empowers you to understand why you will call – to set an appointment. Salespeople often have a tough time contacting potential clients, even though they offer the best 'popcorn'. Without a focused or expected outcome, their form of contacting can scare away the flock! An outcome gives your call a purpose.

Although you can call and talk about anything, dynamic communication must be a constant part of your daily routine. I love contacting because it allows me an opportunity to find new ways to connect with people and set face-to-face appointments.

CONTACTING FOR A CAUSE

You and I have at least one thing in common: we are both in sales. That being said, I constantly look for ways to serve people. Quite often, when you do things for others, many good things come your way. As a former Marine, I have always loved the idea of sharing my programs with the Marine Corps. But what reason would I have to contact the Corps?

Just after my wife was diagnosed with breast cancer, I took an active role in the Relay For Life event in my home town. Relay For Life is the main volunteer-driven cancer fundraising event of the American Cancer Society. I volunteered as the Event Chair and was responsible for organizing the event with the help of my committee. I wanted to make this the most amazing Relay ever and have an impact in the fight against cancer. My goal was to have the Marine Corps Color Guard help to open our ceremony.

I found the number for the Los Angeles Recruiting Station (Prospecting). I called (Contacting), and explained my goal and was given the e-mail address to the Sergeant Major (Prospecting). I e-mailed the Sergeant Major (Contacting) and briefly described what I wanted to do. He quickly replied and confirmed that the Color Guard would be there. I sent him a copy of my book (Follow-Up) and thanked him.

A few days later, he responded and asked, if I would be willing to speak to his Marines. I confirmed and marked the appointment in my calendar. I traveled over 100 miles to Bakersfield, California, and trained over 100 Marine Recruiters on my book, *The GOAL Formula* (Presenting). Since then, I have received numerous book sales from Marines and have been hired to speak at other events for the Corps.

By contacting for a cause, I had a definitive purpose for my call. It allowed a cold call to be received warmly and has led to great friendships with the Marines, allowing me to consistently do something that I love – speak with Marines. Building this aspect of my business was never about selling, it was about serving.

I do not recommend joining a charity organization just to expand your business; it will not work. I do encourage you to be a part of something that has meaning for you and puts you into position to help others.

Remember, contacting is all about setting the appointment. Save your best for your presentation. Have you ever seen a good movie trailer, then rushed to see the movie, only to feel disappointed because 'all of the good stuff was in the trailer'? Do not spoil your presentation with a long trailer. Movie trailers are typically under two minutes! Sound familiar?

On the next page is a template that I use to map out whom I plan to contact, how I will contact them, and the details of results I made. I typically work with two weeks worth of contacting lists in front of me. Many times, a prospect may be so busy that they ask me to call them back in a week. I immediately put them on the list for that day. I often receive e-mail replies asking for a phone call on a specific date – I write it down ASAP.

As you make contact with your prospects today, you will start to build your contacting lists for the upcoming weeks. Your contacting list is important because it gives you a day-to-day account of everyone you made contact with and what your next steps need to be. I have a binder that I keep my list in so I can easily review prior and upcoming weeks.

Contacting enables **Presenting!**

3-D CONTACTING LIST   DATE _____

NAME	TYPE	RESULT

TYPE: E = E–mail   P = Phone Call   D = Drop–By

CHAPTER 6

GEAR 3 – PRESENTING

Moving from content to connection.

Sales presentations come in all shapes and sizes. I have given many and I have observed many more. An unlimited amount of tools exist to help make a great presentation. I have seen PowerPoint slide shows, dry erase boards, flip charts, easels, pictures, videos, and graphs.  Some presenters wear suits, while others wear shorts and sandals.

Some people jump up and down on stage, while others stand as still as a robot. Some were loud; others were barely audible. Some lasted ten minutes while others took more than an hour. I have listened to men and women, young and old. I have listened to presentations in coffee shops, homes, businesses, and stadiums.

Presentations can involve a combination of the above styles. Some use more, while others use less. I have seen presentations succeed and I have seen them fail. Early in my career, I delivered presentations that did not result in any sales, even though I thought I did an outstanding job. In fact, presentations that fail to deliver usually end the selling process at that point.

So what style is the most effective? The best presentation is the one that generates a sale. Every buyer is different. Not every style will work with everyone, so you must find the common ground between you and your prospect. You must be able to build rapport quickly, deliver a meaningful message, and leave your audience wanting to buy. Because your presentation time most likely will be limited, that may seem like a lot to accomplish in one appointment. Welcome to sales!

Salespeople are easily intimidated to make presentations. After all, public speaking is considered by many as their number one fear. In fact, people fear dying less than speaking in public. While there is a lot riding on your presentation, the best ones should be as natural as taking a casual stroll along a beautiful beach. Everyone likes that image, even your potential client.

Initially, salespeople focus 100% of their energy on their performance, not the reaction from the audience. The key is not what you bring to the presentation, it is what your audience leaves with. Your presentation is not a song and dance. It is your opportunity to communicate your belief level in what you offer and demonstrate your personal commitment to your client.

There is a good chance that most everyone you want to sell to has already heard a presentation about similar products from someone else. There is also a good chance that they will hear another presentation about similar products after yours. This chapter is not about presenting your product better. Instead, it teaches you how to present yourself better, which is what your client is ultimately basing their decision on.

When you are presenting, don't look for applause, look for approval.

TYPES OF PRESENTATIONS

To properly turn your Presenting Gear, you must know your client well enough to be able to develop a case–specific presentation that works for them.

Too often, salespeople regurgitate the same presentation material regardless of what type of presentation they are giving. There is nothing more distracting than a one–dimensional presenter. Although there are several ways to deliver your message, I have found that there are really just three types of presentations.

The 3 Types of Presentations:

1. Primary presentations   –   What you offer
2. Proposal presentations   –   What you sell
3. Purpose presentations   –   What you support

I have given many primary, proposal, and purpose presentations throughout my career. Although my focus differs for each type, my desired objective is the same: to generate a sale. Let's take a closer look at each type.

Primary Presentations

This is generally an overview presentation and you will touch on the products and services you have to offer. If you are recruiting for a business opportunity, you will describe the advantages of working for your organization. Many network marketing businesses use compelling primary presentations in their recruiting efforts – they sell the benefit of earning additional income by helping others.

Although this is the first presentation you are making to the individual, business, or organization, it is not the first presentation they have sat through. From the moment you start, they are sizing you up, comparing you to the last presenter who tried to sell them. Your job is to present your material in a way that they have not experienced.

I love primary presentations because there is little pressure about completing a sale. Instead, I am letting them know that they should choose me, even though I may not know exactly what they need, yet. This is my opportunity to talk about the benefits that I bring to the table. I let them know what my company stands for and what they can expect from me. If my presentation is to a small number of people, I will take the opportunity to ask questions throughout to learn what their goals are.

When I make a primary presentation to a large group, and I cannot easily direct the questions to the crowd, I will generally connect with the decision-maker immediately following the presentation. Remember, my primary presentation with the Marine Corps was in front of 100 recruiters. The Sergeant Major, who invited me to speak, introduced me to his commanding officer just before I took the stage. After I completed my presentation, I immediately spoke to the commanding officer to identify his needs. Within a few weeks, he had referred me to his commanding officer who then invited me to speak with another group of Marines.

Proposal Presentations

If you delivered a compelling primary presentation, you will open the door to present a proposal. A proposal presentation is initiated by your prospect because they are interested in buying a product or service. They may also be interested in joining your team, if you offer a career opportunity. Never assume that the people you are presenting to will only be reviewing your proposal. Most people review multiple presentations before making their final decision to buy.

A hard-hitting proposal does not guarantee a sale, even if you have the best price or business opportunity. What stacks the deck in your favor is how well you deliver an exceptional presentation. A buyer can easily show your proposal to a competitor, who made a better delivery. Your competition can quickly make the necessary adjustments to beat your proposal. Great prices can be beat, great presenters cannot.

You are the edge in a proposal presentation, not the proposal itself. Most buyers see the value of choosing the right salesperson and are usually willing to pay a little extra to work with that person. Your presentation is your time to shine!

Purpose Presentations

Purpose Presentations are the ultimate ice–breakers! They are usually the shortest presentations you will make but often have the greatest impact. During these presentations, the audience may consist of many people you do not know. Your presentation, when properly delivered, will convert everyone in the audience into a warm contact, build rapport, and immediately strengthen your relationship with them.

I always invite existing clients and prospects to presentations I make for charity events. As you develop new friends in the crowd, they eventually ask what you do for a living. It is a natural, non–sales transition to letting them know what you sell. If you walked up to the same person in Starbucks and started off with, "Hi my name is Erik, I sell...," you would most likely be shut down before you could finish the sentence.

Too many salespeople have a good presentation. I know that sounds like a good thing, but understand that I said they *have* it. I did not say they *give* a good presentation. Having a powerful slide show or professional flip chart is only a small piece of the equation. If presentation tools could make a presentation pay off, you could simply mail it to your prospect, sit back, and let the orders come in. 3–Dimensional Sales Leaders deliver effective presentations because their delivery adds depth to the content, which allows them to connect with their audience. In fact, most could do it without any tools.

Smart presentations are all about connecting! As a financial services agent, one of the products I sold was life insurance. I know, not the most glamorous product, but it did serve a necessary purpose. In the beginning, when I made presentations, I emphasized the importance of life insurance to both individuals and businesses.

I used the glossy pages in my professional flip chart to stress the value of the products. I backed it up with fact sheets detailing the statistics of life insurance and the benefits of owning the proper amount. But my prospects did not seem to be as excited as I was about insurance. Then I added something to my presentation that moved it from content to connection. That move separated me and my presentation from my competition.

During the life insurance section of my presentation, I would show them a picture of my wife, but not of our wedding or of Gina on the beach. I showed a picture of her in the hospital during her cancer treatments. She was bald and frail, and she was also uninsurable. Gina did not have life insurance prior to being diagnosed. As a cancer patient, she could not qualify for it. And she was only 27 years old.

Sometimes, Gina came with me to meet my prospects. When you present, do everything necessary to deliver your true message! By moving from content to connecting, I sold life insurance to almost every person I presented to. Those who already owned a policy either asked me to replace it or assigned me as their agent of record. Because my presentation created a bond and connected us, they made the decision to become my client.

How can you develop that special connection with your clients? You have a limited amount of time to move from content to connection, so you must focus on two things: Actions and Words.

ACTIONS

You and your presentation will be judged and evaluated in various ways, and many of them will be beyond the words you say. In fact, many of them occur before your presentation even begins. Regardless of what type of presentation you are making, if you drop the ball here, it is tough to pick it back up and score a touchdown during your delivery. Let's take a look at these important factors, so you can stack the deck in your favor.

Be Prepared

Proper preparation will allow you to get to know your client. If you are unprepared, 'know' can quickly turn into a 'no'. Perform the necessary research to make sure that you speak the language of your clients. Just because your presentation went well at ABC Company does not guarantee that it will go well at XYZ Company.

Some businesses are hit harder by current economic challenges than others. If you are speaking to a company that is suffering, do not be oblivious to their plight. On that same note, if you present to individuals, or families, you may be speaking to a person who works for one of these businesses. Understanding the economy and the markets allows you to understand people and their challenges.

Another vital step to being prepared is to practice your presentation. When you are with a client, it is time to present, not to practice! I tend to rehearse many times leading up to my presentation. I meticulously focus on the key points relevant to my specific audience to make sure I do not forget something that would allow me to make the all–important emotional connection. Being natural is paramount, so I make sure to do a rehearsal the night before to allow my mind to work on things while I am sleeping.

Be On Time

Time is a valuable commodity. Never be late to a presentation. Chances are good that the last presenter was on time or perhaps even early. Over twenty years ago, the Marine Corps taught me to be at least 15 minutes early, and I still apply that strategy today.

If you are speaking as part of a group of presenters, I recommend getting there even earlier. I have spoken at many large events that my clients were hosting. When I speak with the Marines, it is usually at an all–day event, with time allocated for a wide array of speakers. I have delivered messages at financial services events and delivered keynotes at corporate workshops. In these situations, I always ask for permission to show up early to hear other speakers and to meet some of the people on their team.

Look Sharp

Regardless of the required attire for the audience, you need to look your best. If you are going to be perceived as a professional, you need to look like one.

Provide Materials

I always leave something behind, especially if I am one of several speakers. The more professional the literature, the more likely they are to keep it. It can be easy to make copies of a handout, but that material usually ends up in the trash. I like to leave a professional, full-color flyer, complete with an endorsement from a client. At a minimum, give out your business cards, even though receiving them is much better than giving yours away. This allows you to expand your prospecting and subsequent contacting.

Expect Obstacles

If something can go wrong, it usually does. A 3-Dimensional Sales Leader is ready for any obstacle that gets in the way. If there is going to be an obstacle, remember this valuable point, it will always happen at the worst possible time – during your presentation. The audience will either witness you struggle to overcome the obstacle or observe as you hurdle it and keep on moving.

When you present at a home, a business, or in a neutral location, you may not have complete control of the equipment. How you handle these kinds of small challenges is a telling sign to your client of how you will handle their business.

Keep in mind that all of this happens before your first word is spoken! Much effort goes into making a great presentation, but a lot more can come out of it. Now, let's *talk* about *talking*.

WORDS

You are prepared, you show up on time, you look amazing, you have professional materials, and you are ready for any obstacle. Now, it is time to do the one thing that most people fear the most – to speak in front of other people. As you take the stage, all eyes are on you.

While your prospects may not remember every word that you speak, they will remember your message. An effective presentation is not about the bells and whistles, it is about the harmony you create. Instead of trying to impress the audience with your presentation skills, move your audience with your connection skills.

To powerfully connect, let's discuss what to say.

Build Rapport

Although your initial warm contact will be at the presentation, cold contacts will be there too – the people you do not have a relationship with. Building rapport immediately is crucial. I always start by thanking the audience for their time and by thanking my warm contact for making this presentation possible. A thank you goes a long way.

I acknowledge the reason I am there. I immediately address any of their goals that I am aware of and how my products and services will help them to accomplish those goals. This step takes very little time, but it paves the way for their complete attention.

Share Your Story

A presentation without a personal story is like a movie without a plot. Even the best special effects won't save you if you fail to include the emotional substance necessary for a connection. The audience must know how much you believe in what you offer. The only way you can do that is by sharing your personal story, your experience with your products and services. My most compelling story was Gina's inability to be insured, and I shared it on every new appointment.

I once attended a sales training event which featured a dynamic speaker. He was not afraid to talk in front of a crowd. He said everything right while he was teaching his sales techniques, but he failed to deliver a compelling story. His content was polished and exciting, but I never felt the connection of how he applied these strategies to his own selling efforts. It is fair to say that the audience did not feel the connection either. After his presentation, he offered his CDs, DVDs, and coaching sessions, but not a single person bought what he was offering. He made a good presentation but was unable to connect with his audience.

Share a Client's Story

If I am going to buy something, I want to hear how a product or service worked for someone else. Your audience is no different. Let them know the positive impact that you had upon one of your existing clients.

Distinguish Yourself

Throughout your presentation, you must let your audience know what separates you from the competition. Your time is limited, so you must establish your expertise on the specific topic you are presenting, not just on the product itself. When I presented on insurance products, I was not the insurance expert, as much as I was the expert on what the benefits of the products were.

Throughout your presentation, give your audience a sense of your credibility in your industry. Do it naturally, by referencing other presentations you have made. This builds credibility and raises your perceived expertise.

Audience Participation

Most speakers are focused on making a winning presentation by concentrating mostly on the things they want to do and say, and understandably so. But, with such a narrow focus, it is easy to forget that there are people in the audience. If you do not involve the people in your presentation, why should they involve you in their business?

Involving your audience requires that you know your audience. Participation can be as simple as having people raise their hands after you ask a question or you can have someone join you on stage for a demonstration. Most people do not like to be called on, but there are always a few that will volunteer. Always have a small gift for anyone who participates and helps you to make your presentation more memorable.

Stay on Target

When you are on a roll, the tendency is to keep going. But a 3–Dimensional Sales Leader knows the importance of completing the presentation on time. It is better to leave them wanting more than to have them checking their watches. Do not get so caught up in telling stories that you forget to present the topic well.

Avoid information overload. Some salespeople bombard their audience with statistics and technical information because they think it makes them sound knowledgeable. You do not have to prove that you are knowledgeable. They would not have allowed you to present if they felt otherwise.

Use Humor

Humor is one of the greatest ways to build a relationship. Think about your strongest relationships. They typically involve a lot of laughter. I love to be around people I can laugh with. A small amount of appropriate humor can help to melt the ice, but too much can build glaciers. Your presentation is not a stand–up comedy routine. It is an opportunity to influence people to buy from you.

Be a Team Player

The role of a salesperson is to be an extension of the client's team they are selling to. I only speak to organizations that I can be committed to for the long haul. If the only purpose of your presentation is to make a sale, it is highly unlikely that you will make one.

A great presentation allows you to connect with your audience, but a 3-dimensional presentation will entice your audience to make you a part of their team. If you are simply trying to make a presentation, that may be all that you accomplish and your potential clients may choose a different team member.

To turn your Presenting Gear, masterfully combine your actions and your words into your delivery. When a client chooses you to be on their team, they expect you to play – to help them to achieve results.

Your presentation is about much more than how your products work, it is about how you work. Have I made sales without presenting? Yes, every so often a sale falls into my lap. But I circle back, to deliver an effective presentation, to make sure it stays.

The quality of your sales presentations often determines whether a prospect buys from you or from one of your competitors. With the proper focus, you can deliver a presentation which will influence and motivate people to take action.

Presenting gives you something to **Set–Up**

CHAPTER 7

GEAR 4 – SET–UP

When the real sales work begins.

Do you know what's more important than making the sale? Keeping it! You promised your prospect the world during your presentation and now it is time to deliver. You have undoubtedly put a lot of work into getting the sale. There is absolutely no need to lose it.

In sales, the real work starts after the sale is made! Yes, after your client says, "Yes!" It takes a great deal of effort to keep your sale on the books, make sure your clients come back to you, and encourage them to send you referrals. Unfortunately, I have seen salespeople make an impressive effort to complete a sale, only to lose it before the ink was dry.

A client's commitment to buy from you is essential to your success. It is the definitive signal to start turning your Set–Up Gear. But for many salespeople, this is when the selling stops and they move onto the next sale. In the fast–paced, highly competitive selling environment, very few salespeople allocate enough time to this gear. Their Set–Up Gear remains still because they do not understand its significance.

Set-up is your ability to exceed your clients' expectations during the completion of the sale, by creating an environment for unlimited growth. Completing a sale is much like planting the seed of a fruit tree. While each seed carries with it the possibility of a bountiful harvest, you must pay particular attention to cultivating it during this crucial phase. There is nothing more disappointing than preparing the soil and the seed, only to experience a lack of growth.

Too much works goes into generating a sale to let it remain dormant. But that's what happens in many cases. To complete a sale, you must understand the true meaning of 'complete'. If your perception of this important concept is not focused, you will struggle to keep your sales.

Many salespeople consider the sale complete once their client gives a verbal agreement, while others use a written commitment as a sign that the sale is final. Some use time periods to consider it complete, often when it has been on the books for a few months. It is not uncommon for others to view the arrival of their commission checks as the signal that the sale is complete.

These are valuable guidelines, but they tend to create a false sense of completion, causing some salespeople to stop working before the work is finished. I have seen salespeople lose clients and business by relying on these unreliable signals. There is no guarantee that your business will stay on the books, even if your clients says, "I guarantee it."

The Set–Up Gear is designed to increase your chances of keeping the business that you worked so hard for, by first establishing the 3–dimensional guideline for a completed sale. There is only one sign that I use to gauge the completion of my sales. Referrals! A 3–Dimensional Sales Leader does not consider a sale completed until they have received at least one referral from their client! Those who refer business to you, rarely remove business from you.

When a client commits to giving you their business, it is based largely on the commitments you made along the way. By focusing on your Set–Up Gear, you will pay particular attention to all of the steps necessary to properly set up new clients and new accounts. Properly completing the sale is not a 'set it and forget it' technique. Your post–sale involvement throughout this process is crucial. Do not overlook this phase, which can easily disconnect the connection you made with them during previous appointments.

SET-UP REQUIREMENTS

Many salespeople are easily accessible to their potential clients before the sale is made, but become difficult to track down after the sale. When your Set-Up Gear begins to slow down, it is only a matter of time until your sales machine stops producing the results you are looking for.

Based on the type of products and services you sell, the set up requirements may differ for your business, after the sale is made. When I sold life insurance, I arranged for blood samples and medical evaluations to be taken by my clients. As a loan officer, I gathered credit scores, a list of clients' assets and liabilities, and information about their work history. When I sold mutual funds, I prepared asset allocations as part of the application process.

In the entertainment industry, many of my clients placed recurring orders and I set up their credit terms, which demanded extra paperwork and at least a week to process. Some of my clients required special pricing, so I needed to create separate discount sheets just for them. Once approved, all information was required to be entered into a database to create their billing information.

In the personal growth industry, many of my clients are set up with a link to purchase my books and a special code to give their team members a discount on their orders. For some clients, I set up special conference calls with a unique phone number and access code.

These are three different industries that I have sold in. Although the set-up requirements were different, they had one thing in common: they occurred after the sale is made. A sale never ends with the handshake, it only begins. Regardless of what I have sold, I have been required to set up specific components in order to complete the sale. To effectively turn my Set-Up Gear, I focused on three aspects.

The 3 Keys to Proper Set–Up:

1. Guide your client
2. Process the sale
3. Gather referrals

GUIDE YOUR CLIENT

The first mistake that people make with the Set–Up Gear is that they try to close the sale rather than complete the sale. Some companies actually have positions called *Closers*, to help their sales force close the business. Note that I used the term *sales force*, because they will do anything to force the client to do business, even if it is not in the best interest of the client.

That is not the type of operation that characterizes a 3–Dimensional Sales Leader. If you need a closing technique or a *Closer* to complete a sale, you have missed the mark.

Do you like being closed? No, neither do I. Never try to close a sale. If you are helping someone to buy a product, which will help them to accomplish their goals, there will be nothing to close. You need to properly complete their sale, and the best way to do that is to guide them through the entire process.

The care and attention you must show a new client is the same that you would do for a newborn child. In the beginning phases of the relationship, you will want to take every step with them. When you let a child take their first steps without your guidance, there is room for unnecessary bumps and bruises.

When you are not available to properly set up your new client's account for them, you create more work for them. You will create the perception that they do not need you or your service. Never assume that they know all of the steps involved with setting up their account or their order. Guide them along the path, every step of the way, until the sale is truly complete – with a referral.

PROCESS THE SALE

Remember this key point about any sale: it is your client's business, not yours. You have only been temporarily entrusted with it. Break that trust, and you lose their business. Develop the trust and you will extend the time you are allowed to be involved. Only the client decides where their business goes.

Processing their business smoothly is important to your client. As you submit their paperwork, to make its way through your processing system, keep them in the loop, every step of the way. Your client will not know your products as well as you do, so make sure that they feel comfortable at all times.

Every company or organization within an industry have slight variations when processing new business. Some applications are one page, while others can involve dozens of documents and forms. My objective is not to refine your system for processing business, just to enhance your system for keeping it. Regardless of the variables involved in processing your business, none of that matters to your client. As their 3-Dimensional Sales Leader, they perceive you as the industry, the company, and the system. They are relying on you to properly set up their business.

If you send the business to your company's home office to be processed, your client looks to you. If you have an assistant handle the paperwork, your client looks to you. But when your client looks for you, can they find you? If they cannot, you can be assured they will find someone else.

When I speak to salespeople they frequently misunderstand the Set-Up Gear. They prefer not to be involved in the processing of the business, feeling it is too time-consuming. To a small extent that is true. But I have never experienced a processing system that is flawless, because no one else in this phase has as much at stake as you do for the success of this sale.

Delegating the steps to processing new business is important for any successful salesperson. I typically delegate much of this work, but I am smart enough to know when to step in. Many salespeople only want to talk to their clients when it involves good news. When there is an issue with an order, most salespeople make the unfortunate decision to delegate. They shy away from personally contacting their client. You make the commission; you make the call.

GATHER REFERRALS

Although I typically gather referrals during my contacting and presenting phases, most of my referrals come as a result of properly completing sales. Clients do not refer people to you if they are not completely satisfied with how you handled their business. Why would they introduce someone to you unless they are certain that this would benefit the other person?

The average person tells three people about you if you did a great job. But that same person will tell twenty–five people about you if you did a substandard job. Because you gauge your performance of your Set–Up Gear on referrals, your ability to work closely with your client during the processing phase of their business is critical. It is not just for this sale, it is for the future sales that they will send to you.

I am always aware of what I am doing, what I am saying, and how I am taking care of my clients, because the greatest compliment in the world of sales is a referral. How you get a referral says a lot about your relationship with your client and how well you turn your Set–Up Gear.

The referral gathering process has three stages:

1. You ask   –   your client does not give
2. You ask   –   your client gives
3. You do not ask   –   your client gives anyway

If you ask for referrals, but do not receive any, it is time to assess your performance. When you ask for referrals and receive them, it is a good sign that your set up skills are heading in the right direction. Continue to turn your Set–Up Gear to increase the amount of referrals you receive.

A 3–Dimensional Sales Leader experiences the joy of gathering referrals in a much different way. Rarely do they need to ask for referrals, because they are already contacting the ones that their clients have voluntarily given them. Gathering referrals in this way lets you know that your relationship is strong and that the care you have shown to your client exceeds their expectations.

If you have not started to gather a lot of referrals, put more effort into properly turning your Set–Up Gear!

CHAPTER 8

GEAR 5 – FOLLOW–UP

The true testament of your commitment level.

When I first started selling, I searched for ways to achieve greater results, as I am sure that you do. I understood that 'no' came with the territory, but I was determined to hear more people say 'yes'. I knew that every buyer had their reasons for saying 'no'. If I could identify these  reasons, I would start hearing 'yes' more often. So I spoke to many buyers, determined to discover these reasons.

What I found surprised me. The majority of people based their decisive 'no' on one key component. Most buyers shared a common complaint – the lack of follow-up. The follow-up abilities of the salesperson was a determining factor in their decision–making process. Not even the most powerful presentation or the most dynamic communication skills will help you, when you fail to turn your Follow–Up Gear.

Some buyers were annoyed that the salesperson did not call them back, while others were disappointed they did not receive information they had been promised. What shocked me was the frequent mention that some salespeople failed to deliver a proposal, illustration, or price bid that the buyer had requested. There was a lack of follow–up and it cost them dearly! A salesperson who fails to follow–up with a potential client is like a fisherman who fails to reel in his catch. Why cast your line in the first place?

Unfortunately, these are not random occurrences. Salespeople fail to turn their Follow–Up Gear because they do not have a proper understanding of

what follow-up is. Follow-up is another word for keeping your commitment. Consistently turning your Follow-Up Gear allows you to communicate your dedication to serve your existing clients and potential clients.

Properly turning your Follow-Up Gear involves various forms of contacting, but this gear has a much different outcome than your Contacting Gear.
The outcome of contacting is to set the next appointment. The outcome of
follow-up is to increase the momentum of your sales activity.

The 2 Types of Follow-Up:
1. Responding to client requests
2. Initiating action

While both types are critical to achieving consistent results, most salespeople make excuses rather than turn their Follow-Up Gear. Regardless of
their excuses, a lack of follow-up is ultimately a lack of discipline – plain
and simple.

Many salespeople ask me, "How many follow-up calls does it take to
complete a sale?" I always tell them the same answer, "Only the last one."
Which one that is, is up to you to discover. I have completed sales after the
first call and I have completed sales after the tenth call. Too many salespeople give up after a certain number of tries. Some people quit after the
third call failed to produce results, while others toss in the towel after the
first call.

Although there are varying statistics on this, most people tend to finalize
their buying decision around number seven! Wow, that's a lot of follow-
up. Yes, that's a lot, but there are sales waiting for you. Do you have the
determination to make the follow-up call that will complete the sale? Do
you know which call that is? Keep following-up until you discover it.

RESPONDING TO CLIENT REQUESTS

Following-up on a client request seems simple enough. All you need to do is to make the call, send the e-mail, or deliver the information, right? With credibility at stake, why do some salespeople drop the ball? There are always plenty of excuses for neglecting a *client request*, but these are merely the symptoms of the deeper follow-up issue – the lack of discipline.

The two most common excuses for not following up on a client request:

1. "I forgot..."
2. "I was too busy..."

"I forgot..."

When you forget about your client, it won't take long for them to forget about you. Your clients expect you to keep their business front and center of your activities. It should be important for you to serve them, not forget them. Salespeople who forget to follow-up on client requests will rarely have many clients to forget about.

"I was too busy..."

No one is too busy to make money. This excuse sends the signal that your client is not your highest priority. Salespeople who are too busy to follow-up, typically do not have that problem for long!

Not keeping a commitment or neglecting to honor a client's request happens frequently, in every industry. I have experienced it first hand, as a client. I once had a pool contractor tell me that he would give me a quote to upgrade my pool filter – I received no call. I waited for weeks to receive information from my tax preparer – I received no information. I once requested a proposal to have my home painted – I received no proposal. If they had they been 3-Dimensional Sales Leaders and continued to turn their Follow-Up Gear, I would have become their new client or remained their existing client.

Salespeople do not start their day trying to discover new ways to sabotage their businesses, but they certainly do just that when they fail to follow-up with a client request. When you stop your Follow-Up Gear, you allow sales to slip right through your fingers and into your competitor's hands. How many of your potential clients are waiting to spend money with you, right now? Unless you effectively turn your Follow-Up Gear, you will never know.

INITIATING ACTION

What do you do when you have turned all of your gears and you do not get the results you expected? You follow up again – to *initiate action*! Most people do not buy from you after you make your first call, or even your first presentation. But many salespeople stop the selling process at this point, using an excuse that is detrimental to the success of their sales career.

The most common excuse for not following up with action is, "I was afraid..."

"I was afraid..."

This excuse is challenging to overcome. Salespeople often stop turning their Follow-Up Gear to avoid being perceived as 'too pushy'. The fear of coming on strong often prohibits salespeople from making the necessary follow-up calls required to earn new business. Allowing this excuse to overshadow your efforts will deprive you of the important benefits of continual follow-up.

Yes, you can be annoying if you call too often just to get a sale. Proper follow-up reconfirms your desire to serve your potential clients. When you follow up, find the appropriate balance between you and your prospects. This can be as frequent as every week, or be spread out over a period of months. The only way to find out the proper frequency with your prospects is to follow–up.

I had sold financial services for nearly five years when I made the decision to turn my sales gears in the entertainment industry. When I first started my new job at the post production company, I knew that increasing the sales numbers would be crucial to my advancement and to my success. Because I had previously worked at another entertainment industry company, I made a list of everyone I knew. My Prospecting Gear was turning.

I started to turn my Contacting Gear and made some calls, letting my warm market know where I was working. Of course, I managed to set many appointments by simply saying, "I would love to get together and tell you a little more about what I am doing now." I made a few primary presentations, usually over a cup of coffee. It felt great to turn my Presenting Gear. My sales machine was operating smoothly and I was confident that my hard work would soon pay off.

I met up with a good friend to tell him more about my new job. We had attended USC's film school together and he recommended that I call his old roommate, who was now an editor for a hit show on Comedy Central. I called him later that day and he invited me for a tour of their studio. During the tour, he introduced me to the post supervisor of the show. A post supervisor controls where their media services are done – the work I was after.

I made a brief primary presentation to describe the services that I offered. The presentation went great and we seemed to hit it off well. But I did not earn their business. He was happy with his current vendor and I was unable to turn my Set–Up Gear! But nothing stopped me from turning my Follow–Up Gear.

To *initiate action*, I contacted him every so often, but not to set an appointment (the outcome of contacting). I followed up with him by sending a quick e–mail or by giving him a call, just to check in and see if there was anything he needed. Although this account belonged to another salesperson, I continued to turn my Follow–Up Gear.

I remained persistent for over two years, until he finally called and said, "I need your help with tonight's episode." I jumped at the chance and we flawlessly completed the work. In addition to handling that order, I had earned the entire show, and became their new sales rep. It took more than two years of turning my Follow–Up Gear, but it had paid off. It always does, if you stay consistent with your follow–up.

That account was worth hundreds of thousands of dollars and they remained my client until the day I left. In fact, the post supervisor and I have remained close friends. My experience with this client taught me a lot about sales and the importance of staying consistent. You can earn business from someone who has a great relationship with your competition, if you are willing to perform the appropriate follow–up.

FOLLOW–UP DEFINES A RELATIONSHIP

Most salespeople stop pursuing a potential client as soon as they hear, "I'm happy with my current salesperson." They may be happy currently, but most clients want to remain happy. When your competitor drops the ball, and they will, you need to be there to pick it up and run with it. By turning your Follow–Up Gear, your potential client always knows that you are available and prepared to serve them.

Below is a graph of the Relationship Wave, an illustration I use to show the status of the client–salesperson relationship. I have found that most of these relationships have ups and downs. Although it is challenging to develop a new client when their relationship with their salesperson is on the High Point of the wave, it is almost certain that you will win them over when the relationship is at the Low Point.

The Relationship Wave:

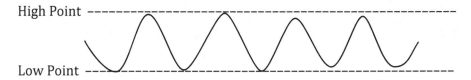

High Point

Low Point

This wave applies to the relationships that your potential clients share with their current salesperson and the relationship you share with your current clients. Follow-up is the key to keeping the Relationship Wave at a High Point. How many of your potential clients are at the bottom of their Relationship Wave with their salesperson? Follow up and find out!

HOW FOLLOW-UP RELATES TO YOUR OTHER GEARS

Turning your Follow-Up Gear ensures that all four of your other sales gears continue to turn. But salespeople often fail to turn this gear in a timely fashion, as it relates to the work they have put into their other gears. Your Follow-Up Gear must start turning as soon as each of your other sales gears begin to move.

Gear 1 – Prospecting: Putting prospects on your list is only as effective as your ability to follow-up with that list. Consistently revisit your list and update your relationship rating.

Gear 2 – Contacting: The outcome for contacting is to set an appointment. That does not always happen on the first call. It may take multiple attempts to get face-to-face with your prospect. Following up with someone, after each contact, lets them know that you are committed.

Gear 3 – Presenting: Follow up with an e-mail, phone call, or a thank you letter for providing you with an opportunity to make a presentation. There is a high likelihood that your competition made a presentation to them as well. Your Follow-Up Gear may be what separates your presentation from your competitor's.

Gear 4 – Set–Up: Follow up regularly with your client regarding the status of their order and/or account being processed, especially if there is an issue. This presents a good opportunity to gather referrals.

Gear 5 – Follow–Up: Follow–up should be mapped out to add the much-needed momentum to keep all of your gears turning! Follow up in a timely fashion with all *client requests*. Follow up strategically to *initiate action*.

Your Follow–Up Gear is designed to turn in unison with your other sales gears. I have seen salespeople follow–up too much and I have seen others follow–up too little. Having the right balance will enhance your ability to turn all of your other gears more effectively.

FOLLOW–UP IS ABOUT TIMING

I am confident that by now you see the need to turn your Follow–Up Gear if you want to achieve greater results. Place a sense of urgency on returning phone calls, sending information, or delivering important documents. When a client request is made, the timing for follow–up is immediate. But not every follow–up situation is so clearly defined. Many salespeople leave follow–up times in the air, creating room for error and dissatisfaction.

When a prospect says, "Call me later," there is a good chance that he does not mean in five minutes. There is also a good chance that he does not mean in five weeks either. It is your responsibility to lock down a time for the follow–up, just as you would an appointment. After all, if a client said, "Come by and make a presentation sometime next week," you would not leave it at that. You would agree upon a date and time and put it in your calendar.

I have had clients say to me, "Call me back next week. OK?" If they fail to be specific with the time they want me to call them, I take the lead. I will reply back with something like, "Not a problem, I'll call you Tuesday at

2:30. Will that work for you?" They will either say 'yes' or 'no'. Once you have the exact time, put it in your calendar.

Once I have the follow-up scheduled, I send a quick e-mail to say, "It was great speaking with you. I look forward to connecting again on (date and time). If you need anything prior to that, just let me know." I follow up after my follow-up calls.

Follow-up keeps your name at the forefront of a prospect's mind. Remember the post supervisor? What would have happened if I failed to follow-up with him over those two years? It is certain that I would not have been on his mind when he needed help. If you do not have a client request to follow-up on, then initiate action, by making well-placed follow-up calls to check in.

Understand that your prospect is most likely receiving follow-up calls from your competition. What distinguishes your follow-up from theirs? Many salespeople follow up by making a call or even dropping by, but most rely too much on the tools of our highly technical world. They choose to send e-mails and text messages for the bulk of their follow-up. All of those follow-up tools can work well, but 3-Dimensional Sales Leaders love to distinguish their follow-up from their competition.

If you want to add a unique flavor to your follow-up, send a hand-written letter or note. The art of adding this personal touch will not go unnoticed. Your client is aware of the time and thought that goes into this level of follow-up. It goes a long way.

Many salespeople ease up on their Follow-Up Gear with existing clients, assuming that their business will always remain on the books. When you fail to follow up, your client may interpret that as a dip in The Relationship Wave. You do not want a client to feel that they are at a low point with you. You know what happens next! If you do not follow up with your existing clients, you can bet that your competition will be following-up with them.

As your other four sales gears start turning, you may not remember to follow up with everyone. You cannot successfully 'wing it' when it comes to follow–up. Too many salespeople like to 'shoot from the hip' in their approach, thinking it will make them appear more natural and less regimented.

You are looking for the 'yes', and the solution to the follow–up problem is simple. I schedule my follow–ups as if they were appointments. I put each in my calendar and treat them just like presentations, or anything else I schedule with a high level of importance.

A Leader's Perspective   Follow–up takes discipline!

YOUR SALES MACHINE

Just as each wave on the ocean is unique, so is each selling situation. Every salesperson sells differently, just as every buyer buys differently. To work your sales machine, regardless of your personal circumstances or the conditions of the market, it is important that you have an intimate knowledge of how that machine works.

3-Dimensional Sales Leaders use their sales machines to help them navigate through a sea of obstacles and challenges successfully. Keeping your five sales gears turning consistently makes it possible to operate in your warm market with people you know.

It takes ten times the effort to develop a new client as it does to maintain an existing one. Turning your sales gears will do more than just create new business. They will help you to keep your business on the books. By focusing on your sales gears, you can systematize your selling efforts, regardless of how complex the sale is. Your sales machine allows you to achieve repeatable, predictable success.

No matter how I generated a new prospect, I always started turning the appropriate gear. Sometimes, a new prospect would be referred to me by an existing client. Of course, the natural tendency is to just sell to them. After all, why start turning all of those gears when the sale has landed in your lap, right?

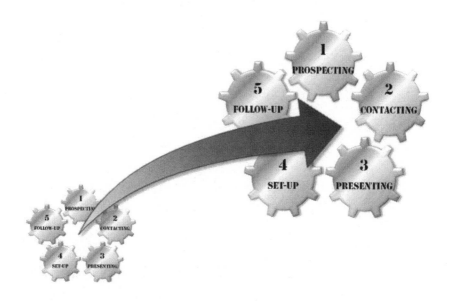

You do not need more sales gears to experience greater results; you need to consistently increase the size of the five sales gears you are already turning. Now let's talk about the 3–dimensional sales knowledge that will allow your clients to perceive you as their 3–Dimensional Sales Leader.

PART III

THE MORE YOU KNOW, THE MORE YOU GROW

PART III

THE MORE YOU KNOW, THE MORE YOU GROW

Sales is not a numbers game, it is a knowledge game.

In the world of selling, there is only one guarantee. That guarantee is that people will buy. Unfortunately, there is no guarantee that they will buy from you. The competition to win the sale is fierce and your competitors will usually not give up without a fight. Salespeople compete, every day; some win and some lose. They strive to stack the deck in their favor, just as you are doing by reading this book. To consistently win more sales, keep your clients, and develop an ever–growing list of new referrals, you must strive to accomplish 3–dimensional sales results.

Most of us remember major events in our lives. I remember the day that Gina and I were married like it was yesterday. I remember holding each of my children on the day they were born. And I remember the day my father passed away. Some memories have such a great impact on our lives that the details never fade. That's how it was on the day when I discovered the power of achieving 3–dimensional sales results.

I was seventeen years old when decided to accompany my friend, Judy, as she drove to the local military recruitment office. She had just enlisted in the U. S. Army and was on her way to drop off some paperwork to her recruiter. I was intrigued by Judy's decision to join the military, and having no solid future plans myself, I was interested to learn more about the Army. Judy's excitement about her new career path was contagious. She had listed off nearly a dozen benefits that the Army offered, before we arrived. Receiving regular pay, eating in the chow hall for free, and living in the barracks without paying rent all seemed enticing.

She also mentioned other benefits, such as using the G.I. Bill toward her college education and using a VA Loan to buy a home. The more she talked, the more interested I became. I had never considered a career in the military until that day. She was so passionate that I felt like I was sitting next to a recruiter. When we arrived at the office, I went in with her, anxious to meet the soldier who had helped her to enlist. But this was not only an Army office; there were recruiters from the other Armed Services. The Navy, the Air Force, and the Marines were all present. The competition was thick!

I stepped into the Army office with Judy and picked up a brochure. She introduced me to the sergeant, who gladly elaborated on all of the benefits I would receive by enlisting in the Army. As their conversation turned to Judy's paperwork, I stepped into the other offices to check things out. Recruiters greeted me, handed me their literature, and tried to sell me on the same benefits Judy was going to enjoy. It did not take long for me to realize that they all offered the same things: the G.I. Bill, the VA Loan, and dozens of other enticing benefits.

Each recruiter explained and emphasized everything I would receive, if I were to enlist in their branch of service. But one recruiter focused less on what I would receive, and more on what I would achieve. With his competition just down the hallway, the Marine Corps recruiter confidently stepped up and shook my hand. He glanced down at the brochures I was holding from the Army, Navy, and Air Force and said, "We have all of the bennies (benefits) too, but we're looking for someone who wants more."

Quickly, I started to think about what I wanted. Perhaps I wanted more, too. "Who do you want to become?" he asked. Before I answered, he asked another question, "Do you think you have what it takes to be the best?" As he handed me the Marine Corps brochure he said, "Not everyone does." As I looked at the brochure, it read 'Marine Recruit Training is No Rose Garden'.

All of the recruiters I met that day appeared to have desire. They were highly dedicated and by the look of all of the ribbons on their uniforms, it was evident that they made the right decisions in their careers. Judging by the number of teenagers coming in and out of their offices, I would venture to say that they were all above-average in turning their sales gears, too.

Surrounded by his competition and offering virtually the same benefits, the Marine recruiter distinguished himself and stood out above the rest. He may have offered what the other recruiters were 'selling', but he presented much more. He asked me questions to find out who I was, who I wanted to be, and where I wanted to go. The other recruiters presented their respective branches well, but the Marine's focus was on getting to know me.

I had arrived at the office to meet the Army recruiter, but on that day, I chose the Marine Corps. It had nothing to do with the 'products and services' I would receive. It had everything to do with the salesperson (my recruiter), showing me a path to my goals. He made me feel great about the decision I made in 1987, and I feel even greater about it today. Judy may have introduced me to her recruiter, but his competition sold me.

On that day, I witnesses two amazing sales results. The first was the Army recruiter's ability to transform Judy into an extension of his sales team. She spoke with conviction and literally took me directly to her salesperson. Do your clients have that level of dedication to you and to what you sell? Do they talk to other people about your products and services with the same passion that Judy did? Keep in mind that she was only seventeen.

The second result I witnessed was the Marine recruiter's ability to separate himself from his competition. He distinguished himself in many ways, but nothing influenced me more than his eagerness to learn about me, unlike his competition. To complete your 3-dimensional transformation, you must strive to achieve 3-dimensional sales results.

3-Dimensional Sales Results:

- Transform your client into an extension of your sales team.
- Continually separate yourself from your competition.

To successfully pursue the path to 3-dimensional results, you must know some things first.

3-DIMENSIONAL SALES KNOWLEDGE

Everyone, including my recruiter, has competition. Regardless of what industry you sell in, someone has the same products and services. Real estate agents compete to sell homes. Life insurance agents compete to sell policies. Office supply representatives compete to sell, well... office supplies. Even most charity organizations compete for donations, despite the fact that they may be raising money for the same cause. What makes them stand out from their competition?

What makes you stand out? In sales, you are only as good as what you know. Knowing your products and services is expected. But that type of knowledge is only a minor factor for successfully selling. I have seen salespeople sell products that they knew little about. On the other hand, I have also seen salespeople fail to sell products that they know everything about.

To achieve 3-dimensional sales results, you must commit to learning the information that will allow you to navigate your sales vehicle to your destination. To do that, you need to acquire 3-dimensional sales knowledge.

3-Dimensional Sales Knowledge:

- Know your Client
- Know your Rivals
- Know your Solutions
- Know your Team
- Know your Plan

The more you know, the more you grow. Systematically building up your knowledge base in these five critical areas will allow you to learn everything you need to know to increase your results. By learning more in one area, you will learn more in the other areas. They all work together to help you to get to the 'yes'.

FIND THE CLUES

Remember, to increase your sales results, you must change your perception about selling and your client's perception about buying. As a 3–Dimensional Sales Leader, I am always searching for the clues that will lead to the 'yes'. I guess you could say that sales work is like detective work.

When you hear 'no', just understand that your detective work is not complete. You may have overlooked a crucial piece of evidence or left that one stone unturned. Too many salespeople quit selling before their investigation is over. Never settle for a 'no' when the trail to a 'yes' is right in front of you.

Many salespeople only search for sales. They miss the vital clues that will allow people to become an extension of their sales team and ensure that they stand, head and shoulders, above their competition. After all, what's better to have: a client or a client who brings you more clients? Without a doubt, every salesperson would love to have a client who brings them more clients. Are you willing to do the legwork to make it happen? Are you determined enough to dig deeper and turn over every stone to find out what you need to know? Or will you allow your competition to do it?

Being a 3–Dimensional Sales Leader is about opening new opportunities. Now let's talk about the tools that you can use to perform your detective duties and achieve 3–dimensional sales results.

CHAPTER 9

KNOW YOUR CLIENTS

Know whom you sell to, not just what they buy.

We all know that having a strong relationship is one of the greatest sales tools available, but many salespeople falsely assume that they know their clients better than they actually do. They make blanket statements about them like, "They love me." Or, "They're not going any-where." Misunderstanding reality can be costly. After all, there were people on the Titanic who said it was 'unsinkable'. There are icebergs in the water, and what you do not know about your client could sink your 'sales' ship!

As a sales coach, I focus on helping sales professionals to increase their results. I typically start by reviewing their prospecting list with them. I am always amazed at how high they rate their relationships. I see mostly '4's and '5's, even though I do not see a lot of sales. Many salespeople believe that they know their clients because they have periodic communication with them. That is never enough to develop a relationship strong enough to avoid the devastating impact of those icebergs.

Influencing people to trust you, to understand you, and to follow you takes time (T.U.F.). It does not happen overnight, nor does it happen after a presentation – even after the best presentation possible. But many salespeople feel that their presentation abilities will take care of their relationship responsibilities.

Most salespeople are trained to talk about their company and explain their products and services in a highly professional manner. They invest much of their valuable time learning how to make a presentation that is natural, informative, and memorable. I have watched salespeople 'knock it out of the park' during a presentation, but they fail to make a sale after the presentation. Equating a great presentation to a guaranteed sale is like assuming that the icebergs will move themselves around your vessel.

You do not sell by only having your clients understand you; you sell by having a deep understanding of your clients. How well do you know the people you sell to? Do you know them well enough to keep them? Do you know them well enough to guard against your ever-present rivals, who are trying to take them? Your clients can become 'easy pickings' for a competitor who knows the information you should know.

Salespeople often judge their business by how well they personally perform. With great detail, they explain the strength of their company, their belief in their products and services, and their commitment to their clients. Typically salespeople dedicate most of their time to helping their clients to understand what they sell, and they use the remainder of their time to understand their clients. In fact, they waste time by asking the wrong questions or using generic information collected on fact-finders sheets.

Although I have sold to people who rate as a '1' on my relationship scale, I work on improving those relationships. And the only way I can do that is to learn more about that person. Getting to know someone is not based on the statements you make, but rather your ability to listen. Asking the right questions and actually paying attention to their answers will elevate your knowledge of them. If you are planning to become 3-dimensional, you need to ask 3-dimensional questions!

UNDERSTANDING YOUR CLIENTS

How would you feel if your doctor began to prescribe medication for you without asking you any questions? Worse yet, how would you feel if your surgeon wanted to operate without understanding what you needed? Neither the certificates on their walls, nor their ability to explain their procedures would matter, if they failed to ask you the right questions. Like most people, you would be looking for a new doctor, one who listens to you and understands you.

Too many salespeople rush their potential clients onto the operating table before making an accurate sales diagnosis. Every gear you turn provides you with an opportunity to learn more about your client and to better develop a strong relationship with that person. If you are only leading your client on a path to your product, you may lose them to a competitor who is leading them on a path to their goals.

Over the years, Gina and I have met numerous doctors: oncologists, radiologists, and surgeons. All were professional and highly qualified. They each made presentations to explain the various types of cancer that Gina had and to help us understand the effects of her treatments. Although I cannot remember every detail of their presentations, I can tell you that we only went back to the ones who took the time to understand Gina the person, not only Gina the patient.

A Leader's Perspective You can only learn about people by proactively listening to people.

YOU HAVE ALL OF THE QUESTIONS

Many salespeople use the *wow* factor to sell, trying to impress their clients with their product knowledge. I prefer to use the *how* factor. I learn what goals my clients have and *how* I can help to accomplish them. When I first started selling, I was more concerned with earning than I was with learning. But it did not take me long to figure out that the more I learn, the more I earn.

To truly get to know my clients, I began to incorporate more targeted questions into my sales operation. There are a million questions you can ask, so where do you start? Initially, most questions revolve around a client's product needs. But as you focus on building that relationship, your questions will begin to center around your client's personal needs – their goals. When you change your focus to their goals, countless opportunities will open for you. When you look for more than a quick sale, you will get more than a quick sale.

Although I had accepted an entry–level position in the entertainment industry, I had the desire to work my way up in the company. One evening, as I was working at the front counter, a customer came in to place a standard order. She had a professional video tape of a documentary film she had made. She only needed a single DVD copy. Right away, I asked her some basic questions about the DVD (product) she was buying as I completed her order form.

But then, I decided to ask another question, even though I was not a member of the sales team at that time. I simply asked her what her project was about. Her face immediately lit up as I showed interest in her project. No longer were we discussing tapes and DVDs, now we were talking about her goals. With much passion in her voice, she told me that the film was about children who had been prosecuted and imprisoned as adult criminals.

The film was called *Juvies* and was narrated by Mark Wahlberg. She told me that she planned to send the master disc that we were about to make for her to a different company that would be replicating thousands of copies for distribution. Her goal was to have the important message in this film reach as many children as possible, and potentially positively influence their lives. What a great goal!

That one question I asked opened up much information about this amazing woman and her project. So I followed it up with another question. I asked, "Do you mind if we bid on the replication order?" She was a long-time customer of my new company, but what she said surprised me. "Oh, I didn't know that you guys did replication," she replied. I was shocked that a longtime customer did not know all of our services. I wondered how many other customers knew of only a fraction of the services we offered.

I told her that we could handle the job and asked if it would benefit her to keep all of her work 'under one roof'. She loved the idea because it would save her much time and effort. Not only did we complete the single, $50 DVD order, but I brought in the replication work as well, which was about $2,500. By asking one question, I increased that particular opportunity by nearly 5,000% and I was not an official salesman, yet.

I may have been entry–level that night, but the questions I asked opened up new opportunities. Within a few weeks, I was leading the sales department; a sales department that was now asking better questions and learning more about our customers. I continued to ask questions and eventually was promoted to Vice President, allowing me to earn a full company override. That commission structure paid me on every sale in the company, not just the ones that I generated. The more you know, the more you grow! Always strive to learn more about your clients.

A Leader's Perspective	Constantly search for opportunities to ask more questions.

YOUR CLIENTS HAVE ALL OF THE ANSWERS

Over the years, the internet has allowed people from all over the world to connect with each other. Some have 'friends' on Facebook, while others have 'followers' on Twitter. People are increasing their opportunities to meet the 'right' person by 'left' clicking their mouse button in the online dating community. Today, connecting with people is easier than ever, but getting to know them is the real challenge.

Each day, I try to position myself to meet more people. But I also try to position myself to grow my relationships. Regardless of what company I have sold for, or what I sold, most of the sales training I had was focused on increasing the ability to present products. That makes sense, but what does not make sense is that so many salespeople struggle to sell. Even with advanced sales training, many salespeople have difficulties countering the objections that their potential clients raise.

Have you ever been faced with an objection from a potential client? I have, even after I made a flawless presentation. Objections are an interesting phenomenon. They all have the ability to slow down our gears and yet they are not real. Rarely do we ever find out the real reasons behind them.

Do these sound familiar?

- "We need to think about it."
- "I am not interested."
- "We already have someone."
- "I need more information."
- "We are over–budget."
- "I'm not ready to buy yet."
- "Business is too slow right now."
- "I don't see a reason to change."

I have sold, despite getting these kinds of objections. And there are many more that a potential client could come up with. While there may be some truth to each one, they are not always 100% accurate. It is your job to discover the real answers.

Over the years, I have found that I dislike all objections, except one. The only objection that I like to hear is the one that my clients say to my competitors. When you operate as a 3–Dimensional Sales Leader, you will redirect objections to your rivals!

RAPPORT LEADS TO RELATIONSHIPS

You do not need a lot of coaching to build rapport with your mom. She is typically a '5' on your relationship rating. If you do need coaching to build rapport with your mom, we need to talk privately. Rapport is the start of any relationship, and like anything in its beginning stage, much care needs to go into its development. Too many salespeople mistake rapport for relationship. While rapport will lead to a relationship, only a strong relationship will lead to the answers you need.

Rapport–building requires keen observation and a good ear on your part. Your potential client may throw out a few rapport–building opportunities, but if you are not willing to listen, you can miss out. You never know when the signal will come, or from what direction. Building rapport will differ depending on the circumstances with your clients.

Here are five rapport–building topics to be aware of when you visit prospects in their environment:

1. Are they married? The ring on their finger may help you with this one. They may also have pictures on their desk or on their walls of their spouse, which leads to…

2. Do they have kids? If so, what are their ages? Your clients usually have pictures and are more than happy to let you know how amazing their children are.

3. Are they a sports fan? Look for posters, team hats, or autographed pictures in their office.

4. What college did they attend? Look for memorabilia from their alma mater. You may know someone who attended the same school.

5. What do they read? Look at the books on their bookshelf to gauge their reading preference. Perhaps you have read some of the same books.

When you meet a potential client at your office or at a neutral location, such as a coffee shop, these clues are not available, so you have to initiate the conversation and casually bring up these rapport–building topics yourself.

I love sports, so I usually mention an upcoming game I am going to watch. If your clients are not sports fans, move on to the next thing. You can try to bring up a time that you had lunch at your favorite restaurant, which usually leads to a discussion about their favorite restaurant – a great place to take them for your next appointment!

You can mention anything from the latest movie you watched to the current book you are reading, perhaps *3–D Sales.* Recommend it to their sales team! Find out where they live, what type of pets they have, where they have vacationed, and what they do for fun.

One of the easiest rapport–builders for me is to talk about the charity work I do with the American Cancer Society. Many people are proudly involved in helping their community and would love to share that information, but salespeople rarely bring it up in conversation.

Building rapport can be a simple, enjoyable process that leads to you learning valuable information about your clients and their goals. Some clients may not be as forthcoming with the information you are looking for, so you must tactfully break down their reluctance to open up. In these cases, I use neutral questions to start the dialogue that will lead to building rapport. Questions such as, "How long have you been with your company?" Or, "How long have you owned your company?" This typically starts the ball rolling.

These questions usually lead into more about themselves, including any companies they previously worked for, or even a different industry they may have come from. It can also lead to other information, such as where they moved from and where they were raised.

No one opens up their lives just because you open up your note pad! Hone your rapport–building skills in order to develop deeper relationships. Most people tend to share valuable information in person, so I strive to consistently set face–to–face appointments.

One great lunch appointment can be worth more than a thousand phone calls! Many salespeople attempt to build relationships over the phone. Worse yet, some feel that they can do it via e–mail. Arranging a face–to–face appointment with a potential client is not always easy to do, but it is worth your time and energy. Get together with your clients and get to know them.

CHAPTER 10

KNOW YOUR RIVALS

Your competition certainly knows you!

There are hundreds of professional sports franchises throughout the world. These teams play in stadiums and arenas packed with screaming fans, who cheer for their home teams and star athletes. At restaurants and sports bars, big screen televisions are surrounded by people

wearing team jerseys, hats and shirts; all cheering at the top of their lungs. People love to watch other people compete and they will pay top dollar for great seats, merchandise, and memorabilia.

But what is the primary focus of any professional sports team? You may think that winning is their objective, but that is only one step toward their main goal: selling. They sell tickets, merchandise, advertisements, and television and radio rights. The bottom line: winning teams sell more! And teams win more by knowing their competition.

Today, nearly 25 professional sports teams worldwide are valued at over one billion dollars. Leading the pack is Manchester United, a British soccer team valued at $1.8 billion. In football, the Dallas Cowboys are valued at $1.6 billion, and in baseball, the New York Yankees are valued at $1.3 billion. In golf, Tiger Woods has a personal net worth that is estimated at over a half billion dollars. Four different sports with one common strategy: Know Your Rivals.

You cannot expect to win if you are not willing to develop a deep understanding of your competition. Before a game, athletes often watch video clips of their upcoming opponents. After losing a game, you can rest assured that the coach will be playing back footage, analyzing their competition, and making the necessary adjustments. Winning is not necessarily about playing better; it is about outplaying the competition.

Being a salesperson is a lot like being an athlete. In sales, too, there is a great deal of competition, occasional screaming and cheering, and usually some shiny trophies. But to be a champion salesperson, you must be able to anticipate the moves of your opponent. After all, the best offense is a good defense. You cannot defend against someone you know little about.

Knowing the rules and regulations of your sales game is never enough to win. You may be the best player the game has ever seen, but if you lack the information needed to know your rivals, you will lose the game. To be a 3-Dimensional Sales Leader, you must have an intimate knowledge of your competition – the people who are trying to take your sales.

How well do you know your rivals? I am not only referring to the company they work for and the products and services they sell! I am talking about the information that changes your sales game and gives you the 'home court' advantage!

THE POWER OF ASKING THE RIGHT QUESTIONS

I once met with a couple to review their financial portfolio, looking for ways to improve the products and services they already owned, and offering several others that they could benefit from. I had made an excellent presentation and my potential clients were already talking about the referrals they wanted to give to me. But there was one small problem. They were not eager to buy the insurance policy that I was recommending.

It was far superior to their existing policy, which they had purchased a year earlier. The company I represented was rated higher than the company they were currently a client of, and my product was less expensive. In fact, it offered more coverage. Did I miss something? I had pointed out all of the benefits and highlighted the advantages of the insurance policy I was offering over my competitor's. And it seemed to be in alignment with their financial goals. OK, what did I do wrong?

I was turning the gears of my sales machine and I was learning more about my potential new clients. I understood my competition's company and his products and services. Why was this sale so difficult? Why were they holding onto an inferior product? I could have easily left their house and chalked it up to 'sometimes people make bad decisions', or some other worthless excuse. But I decided to ask one more question. I asked, "How did you meet your salesperson?" The wife smiled and replied, "He's my brother." Well, there it was – the game–changing information that I needed.

I am not a rocket–scientist, but I was able to determine how high that relationship rated with her. It was so high that she was willing to keep a product that was not helping her and her family to the fullest extent. Your competition can have a strong grasp on your sale, but you do not need to give up. When you understand the necessary information about your rivals you can make changes, both to your defense and to your offense.

I made one final comment and said, "That's great. I'm sure you must be getting the best customer service known to man." I could tell by the look in their eyes, especially the husband's, that they were not getting that level of service, even though their salesperson was a family member. It was evident that they needed a 3–Dimensional Sales Leader, but I needed to break through this relationship barrier. I explained that her brother's company was good, but that he was a *captive* agent, only allowed to sell their proprietary products.

As a broker, I re–emphasized that I could shop from dozens of companies to find products that best suited their needs. I pointed out that I offered financial services that would help them to meet their financial goals. Then I used the most effective sales technique at my disposal; I listened. I listened as they described how strong the relationship was with her brother, but that they were not that happy with his customer service.

Knowing my rival gave me a better understanding of my potential client. Not only did I earn their business, they also gave me many referrals. They even put me in touch with her brother, feeling that it would be better for him to work at my company. As it turned out, he was not planning on staying in the financial services industry. Had I not inquired about my competition, the sale would have easily gone to the next salesperson who came along.

I earned their business because I learned about my opponent. Do not ignore your competition – they are out there, even if you cannot see them. Strive to know your customers better, and do not neglect to gather the important information needed to truly know your rivals. In sales, what you do not know about your competition will hurt your business.

Most salespeople are one question away from earning the sale. But they fail to ask it, typically because that question is not on the pre–formatted fact–finders they are using to gather information. By asking the right questions, you will bring your competition out of hiding. Collecting information about the person you are trying to sell to is crucial. But are you gathering the information necessary to win the client from your rival? How are you learning more about your competition?

SALES TOOLS OFTEN MISS THE MARK

As a sales coach, regardless of what industry I am training in, I like to examine the tools that salespeople use. These tools range from customer relationship management (CRM) software, needs–analysis forms, and interactive presentation resources. Sales tools all serve the same basic purpose: to collect, organize, and present the data required to make a sale. Although these tools help to increase the efficiency of most salespeople, they miss the mark in one area. They pay little attention to the information about your competition.

As the leader of sales teams and sales departments, I ensured their growth by developing an intimate understanding of our competitors. As a 3–Dimensional Sales Leader, it is your job to focus your efforts on collecting this valuable information and using it to increase your sales results. The knowledge that you obtain about your opponents will be instrumental in helping to increase your client base, referrals, and income.

The greatest tool in my arsenal, for gathering this career–changing information about my competition, has always been my fact–finder. Most sales organizations utilize fact–finders, but they tend to focus on collecting information about the potential clients and their product needs. Fact–finders typically lack the necessary space to accurately describe your competition. They often feature one line that reads 'Current Vendor'. You will need to know much more than that about your competition if you plan on winning your sales game.

I have always been crystal–clear about the purpose of my fact–finder: to know my rivals! I have completed hundreds of fact–finders over the past fifteen years and enjoyed the process of gathering the information that allowed me to know my clients better. But I quickly learned that the information a client shares with me, about my competition, is what makes the greatest impact in my results.

To consistently win sales, you must know the 'who', the 'what', and the 'how' when it comes to your opponents.

Discover three key facts about your competitors:

1. Who they sell for   –   their company
2. What they sell   –   their products and services
3. How they sell   –   their techniques

Although some prospects may be reluctant to give any information, most people do not have a problem sharing it about your competitor (their salesperson). They will usually tell you which company the person represents and what products and services they have purchased. Although important, that information is typically not enough to influence a buyer's decision to choose you.

Once you understand whom your competition is, it is smarter to get information about their company, products and services, on the internet. Typically, that information is easy to find online, so do not waste the valuable time you have with your potential clients discussing it with them. Understanding *who they sell for* and *what they sell* is important, but the most important fact is *how they sell*.

How they sell is crucial information because it allows you to understand the sales techniques they used to complete a sale with your prospect. If you understand their offense, you can establish a better defense. Because your competition's techniques are based on their relationships, invest time with your prospect to learn more about the relationship they have with your competition. While not the easiest information to gather, it is the most helpful.

A tell-tale sign that the relationship between your prospect and your rival is strong will be their reluctance to disclose the first two facts: *who they sell for* and *what they sell*. But I would rather know that I have an uphill battle to earn a sale, than to be oblivious to the strength of that relationship.

Regardless of what you call your competition: competitor, opponent, or your arch-nemesis, the only description that matters is what your potential client calls that same person. Do they refer to them as their salesperson, account rep, friend, or even family member? Most people do not instantly volunteer this information. It is up to you to dig deeper until you find it.

When salespeople tell me about a sale that they failed to make, they usually refer to it as a *lost* sale. When I ask them what happened, they generically reply, "Yeah, I lost that one." Or, "That one got away." There is no such thing as a *lost* sale. Sales are never lost, they are merely found by your competition. When you know your rivals, you will be the one who finds more of these notorious *lost* sales.

EXPAND YOUR FACT-FINDER

You need the hard facts, the gems, and the undeniable evidence that will influence people to choose you. The success of your sales career is largely based on your ability to attain the 3-dimensional answers about your competition. And there is only one place that those answers can be found –your prospect. A properly developed fact-finder will elaborate on the answers you need to discover in order to make more sales.

If you are serious about making a sale and keeping that sale, you must know not only *who* the competition is, but you must know *why* your potential clients would choose them. The only way to find out that information is by asking your prospects the right questions. But where do you start? Most salespeople feel uncomfortable to ask these questions on the first phone call or even during the first meeting. But with persistence, you can chip away at the competitive wall that blocks the path to your sales.

Although my fact-finders generally have at least one full page dedicated to questions about my competition, there are five key competitive questions I like to ask early in the relationship.

The 5 Competitive Questions:

1. Which company do you currently buy from?
2. How long has your salesperson been servicing your account?
3. How long have you known your salesperson?
4. How do you know your salesperson?
5. If there is something that could be improved upon, what would it be?

I typically do not break out my fact–finder to ask these competitive questions, even though they are on the document. I prefer to have these important questions memorized, so I can diplomatically work them in at appropriate times with my prospects. As you build relationships, your prospects will eventually begin to share the subtle hints about their relationships with your competitors.

If you need to, ask permission by saying, "Do you mind if I ask you a few questions to better help me to serve you?" I have never been told 'no' to that question and I am usually rewarded with the answers I need. Each piece of information you can get them to disclose moves you one step closer to having them refer to you as their salesperson or better yet, their friend. Review your current fact–finder and take a closer look at the quality of the questions you are asking about your competition.

Investing the adequate amount of time into your relationship will allow you to ask those uncomfortable questions. Over time, as your prospect answers all five questions, you will increase your chance of landing a sale and developing a stronger relationship. If there is any reluctance in answering these questions, your chance of making a sale is more challenging and you will have some immediate relationship–building work to do. Unfortunately, this is when most salespeople toss in the towel and look for an easier sale from another prospect.

There is no website that will give me my competition's relationship information with my prospect. And none of my rivals are willing to share that valuable knowledge with me. Only one person knows the intimate details about that relationship – my prospect. Our job is to get these answers from them. Enhance your fact–finders and make the commitment to get all of your competitive questions answered.

NET'WORK' YOUR WAY TO THE ANSWERS YOU NEED

When I work closely with salespeople, they always want to know what they can do better. Most are willing to consistently turn their five sales gears, but they can not understand why their sales numbers are lower than expected. Their numbers are low because they limit their opportunities to find answers. I attend networking events to position myself in front of people who can provide me with the answers about my competition.

Too many salespeople view networking events, such as industry mixers and client parties, as a way to meet people. That is a 1–dimensional perspective of networking. It is not called netmeeting, it is called networking. You are there to work. It is not only whom you meet, but also what you learn that will enhance your results. Everyone at a networking function is there to meet people, but if you show up just to collect business cards, you miss out on the potential that these events offer.

Regardless of what industry you are in, if you want to sell more, attend events that allow you to connect with more people and ask more competitive questions. It is highly likely that your competition will be there as well. You do not want them to receive the answers that lead to a 'yes', before you do. I have found that people attending these neutral events tend to be forthcoming with valuable information.

After a long day, many people are willing to open up and share their frustrations with you, as long as you are willing to listen. When you take the time to listen to the challenges of your cold market, they do not stay cold for long. Typically, I learn more during a networking event than at several power lunches! But I *work* when I network. I am not there for the food and drinks. I use this time to ask competitive questions and I typically get game–changing answers. Often, my future clients introduce me to their current salesperson – my rival. I never want to miss the opportunity to meet my opponents in person. I love to size up my competition.

If you are committed to developing a 3–dimensional sales career, then focus on increasing your knowledge while you are at these events. Specifically, learn as much as you can about your competition that is not on their website or in their brochures. Although my main purpose for attending networking events is to find answers, I often find many of my competitors *lost* sales at these gatherings. But I never lose focus of my main purpose: to work at discovering useful information. I search for the answers about my competition, which allows me to make more sales.

Salespeople miss out on sales because they fail to get the answers that unlock the bulk of their potential sales. Most people ask non–dimensional questions like, "What do you need?" Or, "What can I do to earn your business?" Instead, 3–dimensional competitive questions will turn your fact–finders into sales detective forms that increase your odds of developing new business. After all, isn't that what fact–finders are for?

YOUR COMPETITION IS EVERYWHERE

Unlike athletes, salespeople do not usually have regular contact with their direct competitors. But, they are out there. If another salesperson is able to win the sale from your prospects you had better make sure you understand why, before more people on your prospecting list move to a client list other than your own.

If you are fortunate enough to have a prospect confide in you about their relationship with another salesperson, always treat that information with the highest level of professionalism. Never speak negatively about your competition. Talking down about a competitor's company, their products, or the actual person speaks volumes about your integrity. It may even show a lack of it.

While most of our competitors sell for other companies, some exist in our own offices. If you work in a sales department that employs several salespeople, you may find your competition sitting at the desk right next to yours. Being on the same sales team can be challenging, but it does allow you to gain an intimate knowledge of your competition. Although you will learn a lot about them, just by observing how they sell, remember the golden rule is not to pluck clients from co-workers.

Instead, sales offices are better served by fostering an environment of cooperative competition among their own salespeople, especially when team members operate within overlapping territories. By keeping the sales goals of the company at the forefront of your operation, you will help to ensure the success of all members of your team.

The best market research, competitive analysis, and product illustrations are no match for a strong relationship with your clients. Invest the majority of your time to build the relationships with them, which in turn, will provide you with the answers to your competitive questions and will allow you to complete more sales by getting to know your rivals.

CHAPTER 11

KNOW YOUR SOLUTIONS

People do not buy you.

What is the single greatest factor that influences a person to consistently choose you as their salesperson? Before you answer that question, take a closer look at it. I hope you noticed that I did not say to 'try' you as their salesperson. Most salespeople have been 'tried' out by a  client or two. I am talking about retention; continually being chosen over your competition. Like most salespeople, I know that you have a deep desire to understand that all–important quality that affects someone's decision to choose you.

Is it your education, your experience, or your job title? Those are nice. Could it be your knowledge of the products and services you sell? Certainly that helps. Perhaps it is your pricing, your turn–around times, or your promises. Those are strong points too. I know, it must be having strong endorsements from other buyers.

The answer is not found on your resume, your website, or even in your presentation. In fact, the answer has nothing to do with the above–listed qualities. Although they do play a part in opening the door for you, I have kept most clients without any of those being a major contributing factor. I am referring to the common denominator that all clients place value on when it comes to staying with me. As a matter of fact, isn't that what you're looking for too?

There is an old adage that 'people do not buy products, they buy you'. There is some truth to that, but I understand that the 3–dimensional translation is that 'people do not buy you, they buy your solutions'. They buy the way you conduct business, the way you react to their needs, and the way you solve their problems. If you stopped finding those solutions, your clients would stop choosing *you*. You are only as good as the solutions *you* provide!

Your solutions keep the door open to your customers. Although I recommend building strong relationships, your clients do not even have to like you, as long as you are providing viable solutions for their business. Yes, I have had some particularly unfriendly clients with less–than–desirable people skills. Perhaps you can relate. Although I was never certain how much they liked me, I was confident that they loved my solutions. Not every client is looking for a new friend, but every client is looking for a 3–Dimensional Sales Leader who consistently delivers solutions.

Some salespeople fall into the trap of thinking that their clients choose them because they like them. That leads to the incorrect assumption that their clients will be with them forever, regardless of what circumstances come up. It is not difficult for a client to leave a salesperson who holds onto the antiquated 1–dimensional 'people buy you' mentality. They typically leave them for a 3–Dimensional Sales Leader. Now, let's talk about delivering your solutions.

PITCHING SOLUTIONS

I once coached a group of sales agents and executives to help the owner of that company to achieve his goal of increasing sales results. During the first meeting, I asked each of the ten people to take out a pen and paper and briefly describe what their company offered, in two or three sentences. Because this was the group of front–line leaders, I wanted to know how they would make a pitch to a potential client. As their pens frantically scribbled across their papers, some of them looked up at the ceiling, deep in thought, while others scratched their heads. Two people actually crumpled up their papers to start over. After two minutes I asked them to stop.

I gathered each of the papers and read them to the group. Although there were a few similarities in their descriptions, most of these pitches sounded like they were describing different companies. One of them was not even completed. Their pitches gave me a basic understanding of what they sold, but not one of them sparked my interest to learn more (as a potential client). And these were the company's top people!

The average major league baseball pitcher throws the ball at 90 mph. At that speed, it takes less than one second to leave his hand and cross home plate. The pitcher has one objective: to strike out the other player. When a salesperson makes a pitch, they have an objective too. It is not to strike out the client, but that is what tends to happen with most sales pitches. There is an inherent problem with making a sales pitch – most people do it wrong! They strike themselves out!

Although they may take more time to make their pitch than a major league player, when it is done wrong, the 'strike out' happens at roughly the same speed – less than one second. When your client strikes out, so do you. When you pitch a client, you want them to hit a home run, or better yet, a grand slam! Why do so many salespeople throw bad pitches? Salespeople miss the mark by focusing their pitch on their product. A pitch has one purpose – to spark the client's interest!

Your prospect or existing client already has a basic understanding about the product you have, so why waste your pitch–time presenting it? When you pitch a product your chances of striking out go up significantly. When the opportunity comes up for you to make a pitch, make it count.

How do you reply when someone asks you, "What do you do?" What is your response? Most salespeople say the wrong thing, focusing on a sales pitch when they should be delivering a *solution* pitch. Start planting the seed about your solutions from the moment you are asked that golden question, "What do you do?"

Like you, I meet many new people each day. I have small window of opportunity to make my pitch and to spark their interest. If I only have a brief time period to explain what I do, I want them to immediately know that I offer solutions. Yes, I sell books, speaking engagements, and coaching sessions, but people would rather hear about solutions than sales. From the beginning of my conversation, my new contacts understand that I focus on solutions; solutions that benefit them and their businesses.

I must immediately spark the interest of anyone who asks me, "What do you do?" I pitch this solution, "I help individuals, businesses, and organizations to increase their results by accomplishing goals; not just professional goals, but personal goals as well. In fact, I even train the U. S. Marine Corps to accomplish goals, too." My pitch is less than thirty seconds and I typically get the response, "How do you do that?"

That question naturally allows the client to shift me from pitching to presenting. You do not have a prospect's ear for long. A solution pitch will extend your 'air–time' with them.

Most salespeople can describe what they sell in thirty seconds. Can you effectively describe your solutions and peak someone's interest in thirty seconds? Add value to your dialogue by letting your prospect know that your focus is solutions.

Solutions benefit your clients; sales benefit you. What do you think they want to hear more about? Pitch what they are interested in and you will get the results you are looking for. When you have thirty seconds or less to explain your business, throw the right pitch.

Take some time and write out your best solution pitch. It may take time to fully develop it, but keep working on it until you are able to master it. Try it out on someone who knows what you sell, like a friend or family member. With a powerful solution pitch you will be better prepared to talk to more people, spark interest, and achieve results.

DELIVERING SOLUTIONS

Pitching solutions is one thing; delivering solutions is an entirely different ball game. But that's the game you need to win; that is the game your clients will buy season tickets to, year after year. I have listened to salespeople from every industry promise 'the best prices', 'the best products', and 'the best service'. Guaranteeing everything they think a client wants to hear, salespeople sound convincing and sincere as they win new business. But to keep their promises, they must deliver.

Solutions are never delivered with generic promises; they are delivered with three consistent actions. These are the actions that your client uses to compare you to your competitors.

Your solutions are delivered by:

- Your Style   – how you sell
- Your Attitude – how you react
- Your Resolve – how you fix

Keep in mind that your solutions are far more important than the sum of your products and services. During challenging times, which you may experience with your clients, your products and services will rarely be tested; it will be your solutions that will be on trial. Will there be enough evidence for your client to continually choose you, or will they choose your rival?

A Leader's Perspective   Deliver your solutions consistently to keep the door open to new opportunities, even when there are challenges.

Your Style: *is it better than your competitors'?*

Selling should never stop. It should be a consistent part of any client relationship you have. After all, you want to have clients who place new orders, utilize new products and services, and send you more referrals, right? They will only do that if they like your style. Your selling style is one of the first comparisons that a client will make between you and your competitors. You may not understand the difference between your style and theirs, but your client does!

Everyone sells with a slightly different style, regardless of their products. Doctors have their own styles too, different ways to present solutions to their patients. Most doctors are highly educated and trained. But people do not come back to them, or refer people to them, based solely on their credentials. Patients are influenced by their doctor's style. My wife never chose to go back to a doctor because of his credentials. Her decisions were based predominantly on his style; how he presented her with his life–saving solutions.

Every salesperson needs to focus on developing their own personal selling style. But what is a selling style?

> **Selling Style**   –   your unique ability to connect people with the products and services that meet their needs.

Most salespeople tend to adopt some form of *closing* technique as their style. The old 'A.B.C.' style is one of the most popular; not with clients, just with one–dimensional salespeople. 'Always Be Closing' is the style of choice. Why in the world would you have a style that has the word *close* in it? What exactly are you trying to close?

Some salespeople try to *hard close* the sales door, using a heavy–handed approach to close a sale, even though it may not be the right fit for their potential client. Hard–closers usually have many dissatisfied customers and a backlog of cancelled business. Other salespeople favor a *soft close* style, using a timid, 'I don't want to bother them' approach after they have made a presentation. Soft–closers often fail to sell anything, even though their product would have truly benefited their potential client.

If you have to focus on *closing*, then it is fair to say that you must not be very good at *opening*. Closing techniques have a tendency to put an unwanted distance between you and your client. I prefer the 'A.B.O.' style – 'Always Be Opening'. I want to open up dialogue with my clients, open more relationships, and open new opportunities. My personal style is to open up more possibilities, therefore my sales door never closes. It is open for more business from existing clients and additional business from new clients.

Your products and services will not sell themselves; that's your job. The style you adopt will help you to connect with people and retain more clients. Over the years, I have met many salespeople with a wide array of selling styles. Each style was unique; some effective and some less effective. Selling styles reflect the salesperson's *level of service* that they provide to a client.

Identify your level of service in order to help create your unique selling style. There are four service levels that salespeople focus on. The sharper your focus, the greater your results! We all start at #4, but a 3–Dimensional Sales Leader strives to be #1.

The 4 Levels of Sales Service:

1. **SOLUTION SELLING**
2. **CONSULTATIVE SELLING**
3. **COMPETITIVE SELLING**
4. **COMMODITY SELLING**

4. Commodity Selling:

The initial focus of all new salespeople. They react to customer requests and primarily sell on cost. They strive to get the best prices and the best deals for their clients. They are the order takers!

3. Competitive Selling:

As a salesperson becomes well–versed in their own products and services, they become aware of what other salespeople have to offer. As they gain an intimate knowledge of their rivals, they focus on outselling their competition. They look for a fight!

2. Consultative Selling:

Salespeople who operate at this level have the ability to provide value to their clients. They have now developed a deeper understanding with their clients and no longer sell just for today, but consult with them for tomorrow. Clients seek out consultative salespeople to help with the decision–making process!

1. Solution Selling:

Clients look for this type of sales leader. At this stage, you not only consult with your client, but your solutions have positioned you to become an extension of their team. They involve you in much more than just their orders.

A Leader's Perspective　　Solution Selling typically provides up to 80% of all sales revenue.

I have often been told, "I like your style." That is not only a meaningful compliment, but it is a good sign that I am on the right track. If a client feels good about your style, they will repeat the buying process with you and encourage others to do the same. The number of referrals you receive is another good indication of how much people like your style.

As you develop your style, make sure that you remain believable and genuine. Clients have the unique ability to sniff out a fake. Just because you believe in the product does not mean that your client believes in you. Your style will help to convey to your client what you truly offer.

Your Attitude: *is it better than your competitors'?*

Your clients are not always going to have the best day. They may vent to you, or they may even take their frustrations out on you. How you react to your clients will affect their decision to stay with you. Your attitude goes a long way. When your clients experience challenges, or simply have a rough day, you are the beacon of hope for them.

Just as a lighthouse best serves its purpose on a dark night, you are most needed, by your clients, during their tough times. It is easy to have an uplifting attitude when your client places a new order or sends referrals. But what happens when your client cancels an order, needs a price reduction, or fails to return your call? How bright does your light shine at that point?

You cannot hide your true attitude. It will come out in two ways:

1. Your communication
2. Your body language

Some salespeople tend to do whatever it takes to get the sale. They have the biggest smile on their face and are more than happy to bend over backwards at every request. But once the deal is done, they may convey with their attitude that they are done. Clients typically need something after the sale is made. Some need more; some need less. They may call to ask you a question. They may call to receive a better understanding of something. They may call just to talk.

How do you communicate with your client, when they are no longer your prospect? Many salespeople lose clients because they cannot consistently deliver the same pleasing attitude they had in the early stages of the relationship. I have actually heard salespeople verbalize their frustrations with their clients; over the phone and in person.

If your attitude makes people even the slightest bit uncomfortable to speak with you, they will stop calling you. That call will quickly go to your competitor. Be mindful of the words coming out of your mouth; your clients certainly are.

Did you know that there are thousands of distinct languages in the world? Although most people will never be able to speak a fraction of them, there is one language that the majority of people understand – body language. Does your body language convey confidence, credibility, and approachability? Your body language often says more than your verbal skills do about your attitude.

I will be the first to acknowledge that some clients may push you to the edge, but you must maintain a positive attitude. Just because your client is having a bad day does not mean that it needs to ruin yours.

Keep a positive attitude for two reasons:

1. Allows you to stay in control in any situation.
2. Allows you to stay focused on your clients' needs.

Be grateful that your client is seeking help from you. The easy fix is that they take their needs elsewhere. But what would that do to your attitude? Your attitude is such a vital part of your solutions. Learn to keep it high, especially when your clients need it the most. I have received more thank you notes based on helping my clients with an issue, than helping them to place an order!

Your Resolve: *is it better than your competitors'?*

Your customer service skills may be noticed by your clients during the good times, but they are truly tested when there is a problem. And there will be problems. Some you can control, others you cannot. Either way, your ability to resolve issues, in your client's favor, will be a determining factor in their decision to stay with you.

Problems can be ranked on a scale of '1'–'10', '10' being the worst. Each client is different, so a '1' for one client, may be a '10' for another client. It does not matter if you have a home office, account rep, or a personal assistant; the problem is always your responsibility, even if it is not your fault.

Problems originate in two ways:

1. From your client
2. From you

I take a 3–dimensional perspective of problems. I view them as obstacles that I must solve. If the obstacle comes from your client, this is the perfect opportunity to show them what they are paying for – your solutions.

This is when you will understand that clients do not buy you, they buy your solutions. When an issue arises that is caused by your client, it could be due to a lack of or incorrect information they provided to you. This has happened more times than I can count. Sometimes the extent of the mistake could cost your client their job.

I once received a purchase order from one of my clients. She had sent my company a series of cable television shows, on video, to be transferred onto high–definition tapes. The order was valued at nearly $20,000. Everything was processed correctly. Every 't' was crossed and every 'i' was dotted. We even completed the order ahead of schedule.

Then I received a call from her boss, who was also her good friend. He had been instrumental in switching their account to us a few years back and asked me for a 'small' favor. He wanted me to erase this order and not bill them for it. My contact had sent us the wrong shows, and this was not her first time doing it. We were not at fault and deserved to get paid for the work. We would have been justified in send them the original bill.

But her boss was trying to save her job, which gave me an opportunity to present a delicate solution to the problem. I recommended that we hold the copies and use them for another order. We would be able to erase them and re–use the stock. I also told him that I would be required to provide an explanation for the voided order, so I needed to present something of value to my boss.

This was a large company and they did business with a few of our competitors. By offering a $20,000 solution, I was able to get the commitment for nearly $100,000 of their editorial work. We kept our client happy, and I used this opportunity to increase our sales.

I have had plenty of obstacles to overcome that were my fault but not due to neglect. I have had insurance policies arrive with the incorrect amount of coverage, even though I completed the application correctly. I have had media services delivered to a client with a one–pixel glitch on it, caused by the equipment we used to process the order.

Try to look at every obstacle as a way to improve your relationship with your clients. Even mistakes that are your fault can provide you the opportunity to strengthen your relationships. But understand that the obstacles resulting from your neglect are very difficult to overcome. If you are the type of salesperson who pays little attention to detail, you will not have to worry about having obstacles to overcome for long. That client will find a different solution.

Occasionally, my own team members, home office, and assistants have made mistakes. It does not matter how the ball gets dropped, it is up to you to pick it up and run with it before your rival does! This is why I focus much energy on developing strong relationships with my clients. The stronger your relationship is, the less impact an obstacle will have on their decision to continually choose you.

The more business you do with someone, the greater the chances are of experiencing a challenge. Clients do not leave you because of obstacles; they leave you because you failed to deliver a solution to fix the problem.

Make the personal commitment to gain knowledge and sell solutions!

- You sell products — learn them
- People buy solutions — deliver them

CHAPTER 12

KNOW YOUR TEAM

Selling is a team sport!

When I was twelve years old, my family took a trip to Northern California. We stopped in San Francisco for the better part of a day to see the sights. A tour boat took us into the Bay, around the island of Alcatraz, and past the Golden Gate Bridge. At Pier 39, we checked out the shops, enjoyed the food, and wrapped up an amazing visit.

But there was something I liked better than all of the famous landmarks and stores. I loved the street performers. There were jugglers, a few dancers, singers, and even a lady who performed a sword–swallowing routine. But my favorite act was the one–man band. For a quarter, he would play almost any song on his instruments: guitar, harmonica, drums, accordion, symbols.

I must have put at least three dollars into his hat before we moved on. It was so entertaining for me to watch him play his instruments harmoniously. As I matured, my appreciation for music grew and I began to enjoy the harmony of a professional orchestra. Talented musicians, led by a professional maestro, will perform symphonies that will spark your emotions and inspire your soul. The orchestra operates in perfect harmony to achieve the desired results. Does your sales team produce results like this for your clients?

The more I work with salespeople, the easier it is to identify one of the common weaknesses within their operation. They perform much like the one-man band who entertained me as a child, but they never discover the true harmony of being part of a team. Salespeople who try to do everything themselves limit their total effectiveness as a sales leader. They may have good intentions, but remember that clients are not paying for your intentions; they are paying for your solutions. Valuable solutions are nearly impossible to deliver unless you have the support of a strong team.

A 3-Dimensional Sales Leader understands how to achieve better results by being a part of a team. But there is much more to being on a team than being surrounded by talented people. It is about creating, developing, and maintaining a mutually beneficial support system that enhances your ability to deliver your solutions. Whether you are the only salesperson or the member of a sales department, your team will provide you with support and reenforcement. As a team member, you will have more time to pursue sales opportunities through cooperation. But every team needs someone to lead it. That is where you come in.

Clients never pay for a one-man band, especially when they have the opportunity to benefit from a full orchestra. To effectively sell, you must know your team, starting with your position on that team. If you fail to function as a 3-dimensional member of your own team, do not expect your potential clients to ask you to be an extension of their team.

WHO IS ON YOUR TEAM?

Salespeople typically see the benefit in developing strong relationships with their clients, but forget about the people who help to complete the work, process their business, and provide support – their team! Too many salespeople act like the Lone Ranger, often ignoring the efforts of Tonto! That is a mistake that can cost you dearly. Trust me on that one! Behind every great salesperson is a great team.

When I sold financial services, I met with potential clients to review their financial portfolios. I made presentations and explained my illustrations and proposals. I was usually by myself when they signed the application.

But I never made the sale without the help of my team. The efforts of many people on my team allowed me to deliver my financial solutions. My team included my assistant, branch office manager, compliance officer, product providers and their staff, my broker–dealer, the home office crew, and the product experts in my office who reviewed my materials before I went out in the field.

When I sold media services, I met with potential clients in our facility to conduct tours. I asked about their media needs while showing them our technical capabilities. I was often by myself when they told me that I had earned their business. But again, I never made the sale without the help of a team. The efforts of many people allowed me to deliver my media solutions. My team included my facility manager, department supervisors, account representatives, schedulers, accounting staff, technical advisors, engineers, and our concierge.

Whether they acknowledge it or not, salespeople rely in many ways on the efforts of many people to help process business through their systems. Unfortunately, too many salespeople walk around like an Egyptian Pharaoh, rather than a member of the team. If you fail to dedicate the necessary time into developing your team, you will not optimize the contributions your team. The relationships I developed with my team members were as important as the relationships I developed with my clients.

In fact, when I sold media services, I used many vendors to help me complete the order that my clients placed with me. To deliver my solutions, I rented equipment, used delivery services, and ordered video tape stock. In the eyes of each vendor, I was their client. In my eyes, they were valuable members of my team. Instead of barking orders at them, I developed relationships. More often than not, one of my clients would place an order with a near–impossible delivery time. If I did not have enough stock to complete the order, they would have gone elsewhere.

Because I considered vendors as part of my team, I had a smooth working relationship with the owner of a tape stock company and his team. He would make special deliveries to help me complete my orders, sometimes sending me that one piece of stock that meant the difference between success and failure; between commission and cancellation! He could have easily, and justifiably, told me that his driver had left for the day and they would have to send it on the next run. If he was only a 'vendor', I could have easily missed the opportunity for nearly $250,000 worth of additional business. It is essential to know your team!

Who is on your team? If you cannot answer that, let me help you. Anyone who allows you to consistently deliver solutions for your clients is on your team. The efforts of your in-house and extended teams directly affect your results and your income!

WHAT IS YOUR ROLE ON YOUR TEAM?

I have sold for small companies and I have sold for large firms. I have sold to individuals and I have sold to businesses. I have worked in small sales offices and I have worked in huge sales departments. I have sold one–time media services and I have sold long–term financial products. Every situation was different, except for one aspect. I have never sold alone. I may have been the only team member in the field, but I always had a definitive understanding of my role on my team.

Most salespeople want to experience the benefits that a great team can provide, but fail to fulfill their personal obligations to that team. Some try to do too much, like the one–man band. Others do not do enough, failing to even pick up an instrument. They behave more like an audience member, watching from afar, rather than participating in the process.

As a 3–Dimensional Sales Leader, your role is self–explanatory. Remember, a sales position should be a leadership position. Your role is that of a leader. Regardless of what position you hold within the company, you need to exhibit strong leadership traits. It does not matter if you are a sales associate, a sales manager or the vice president of sales; your primary role on that team is to be a *leader*. More specifically, you are a 3-Dimensional Sales Leader.

There are many books on leadership because it is the foundation of all successful organizations. Is it the foundation of your sales operation? It should be. Every team needs a strong leader to ensure that all team members are on the same page. I recommend that you lead the people and manage the work.

The primary reason that leadership is such an essential component is that sales teams require precise communication at all times. The number one quality of an effective leader is communication. When you analyze every mistake that has happened in your sales career, or every obstacle that has occurred, you can most likely attribute it to a break-down in communication. 3-Dimensional Sales Leaders focus on eliminating this breakdown.

What would your results be like if you had a team of leaders, focused on effective communication? I would venture to say that it would be 3-dimensional. I am confident that your clients will see the difference, too. Communication and selling go hand-in-hand and your leadership skills will ensure that they are inseparable. When you help to make the workload of your team flow, your team will help to make your selling efforts flow.

TRANSITIONING THE WORK

I will be the first to admit there were salespeople in my offices with broader product knowledge than mine. Regardless of what industry I sold in, there was always someone who had a better understanding of the items on our 'menu'. But no one could orchestrate as effectively as I could, and that is why I always had much more to orchestrate than they did.

To process new business for your clients, a great deal of important information has to be shared amongst the people on your team. Often, your clients may send the information directly to you. It is your responsibility to ensure that their information is transitioned properly. As a 3–Dimensional Sales Leader, your proficiency in transferring information will lead to more and better sales.

Your ability to handle many tasks at once will have a direct impact on your success. By creating a team of 3–Dimensional Sales Leaders in the media industry, our production numbers shot through the roof. We experienced many months of exponential growth, with increases in sales of 60% to 100% per month. Our sales growth was a direct result of our team work – transitioning information. To keep the business that we were bringing in, we developed a stronger team, not just a bigger one.

To encourage more effective transitioning of information amongst team members, I implemented a system called O.D.S. with our leaders.

The O.D.S. System:

- **Orchestrate** the project.
- **Delegate** the tasks.
- **Supervise** the performance.

Many salespeople experience growth in their business, enjoying time periods of more sales, more clients, and more revenue. Unfortunately, they rarely see corresponding growth of their teams. If your team does not grow with you, sustaining growth will be difficult.

Your job is to orchestrate. Remember the maestro? Get your team onto the same page, if you want to hear that sweet sound of success. Too many salespeople lose their clients because they are unable to handle the volume of new business. They often put much effort into developing new clients, but fail to put adequate effort into developing their team.

Regardless of what you sell, you can take the same approach and achieve the same results. Implement the O.D.S. System in your organization because your team is essential to your success!

OWNERSHIP MENTALITY

As I worked my way up at the post production company, I wanted to develop repeat customers, which would develop repeat commissions for me. Although the company had a good track record, they had nearly 15% of their work returned due to minor errors, usually the result of a misunderstanding among team members. As a leader, I understood that the solution would not only be found in our ability to communicate, but in our ability to recognize the efforts of our team members. Appreciation goes a long way!

Many people try to improve the effectiveness of their team by asking their team members to adopt an *ownership mentality*. In other words, they want each person to act like an owner; to treat every situation exactly like the owner would. I agree with this approach, but there is one problem. Owners view things with a unique perspective because they benefit, usually financially, when things are done correctly.

How does your team benefit? Do not expect them to have an ownership mentality for long, if they do not have an ownership benefit as well. Recognizing the efforts of your team can come in many forms. In order to show my appreciation for a job well–done, I have awarded plaques, trophies, gift certificates, and hi–fives! Yes, a pat on the back and a 'thank you' go a long way. But is that what motivates you? I am fairly certain that you are not selling to receive a shelf full of trophies.

In order to reward team members who acted like owners, I implemented a plan to pay them like owners. Working with the owner of the company, we introduced a commission structure to reward them on all orders that were completed correctly. Based on your industry and the company you sell for, you may not be able to do something exactly like this. But as a leader, it is your job to develop procedures that will recognize team members and give them incentive to act like owners.

As a result, the error ratio in that company dropped from 15.0% to 0.34%. That is less than half a percentage point! Our clients were happier, our team members were happier, our sales team was happier, and the owner was happier. We created a win–win scenario within our own team by launching the type of recognition that fostered an ownership mentality.

TEAM MEETINGS

Most people dislike meetings. Why? Because they are usually conducted to discuss what went wrong, specifically, what they did wrong. I would not want to go to that type of negative gathering either. I prefer to attend meetings to discuss what is going right. Energetic, optimistic, growth-oriented meetings are the best way to increase communication, develop team camaraderie, inspire commitment and recognize the efforts of individual team members.

Scheduling regular, proactive meetings will eliminate the need for the morale–busting meetings people dislike. As a 3–Dimensional Sales Leader, you will increase sales, which in turn, will increase your team's workload. It is up to you to make every effort to coordinate and lead high–energy, positive, exciting sales meetings to help complete all orders and achieve the expected results.

Orchestrating a 3–dimensional sales meeting cannot be taken lightly. This is not a time to hear yourself speak. Do not waste time. Your meetings should be brief, be informative, and be inspiring.

The 3–dimensional components of an effective sales meeting:

- Present current numbers
- Discuss upcoming projections
- Share success stories
- Announce new goals
- Recognize 3–dimensional efforts

Present Current Numbers: Your team must know where they stand at all times, if you want them to get to where they need to be. Have a *scorecard* to show the growth you are achieving in your sales numbers: weekly, monthly, quarterly, and annually.

Discuss Upcoming Projections: This is when team goals are discussed. If the team knows what type of work is coming, they can better prepare for it. It also allows them to better understand the effort of each person. Allow the dialogue to flow between the leaders on your team. This type of communication is necessary. It eliminates the ever–popular excuse of 'I didn't know'.

Share Success Stories: Salespeople and key team members must share their success stories. When they tell others how they developed a new client, resolved an issue, or earned a referral, it will do much more than lift everyone's morale, it will also inspire others to strive for success.

Announce New Goals: When new goals are announced in a meeting, it will create excitement about the future and a clear purpose for the team. New goals cause new commitment levels and encourage others to take more action.

Recognize 3–Dimensional Efforts: This is the best part of any meeting. Recognizing people in front of their peers encourages everyone to do what it takes to be recognized as well. It also lets people know that you actually care about them, not just what they can do for you.

The best sales meetings often involve more than just the salespeople. By including extended team members, such finance or production personnel, in these 3–dimensional sales meetings, it raises the bar on the overall performance and the results of everyone in attendance. The differences between average salespeople and 3–Dimensional Sales Leaders can easily be discovered by analyzing the caliber of their team.

A Leader's Perspective   You can try to sell by yourself, but if you want to create consistent, long–term sales results, know your team.

CHAPTER 13

KNOW YOUR PLAN

The instructions to building a great career.

I once coached a salesperson who was struggling to reach his numbers, but he could not figure out what he was doing wrong. He was energetic, passionate, and had no fear of talking to people. Trust me, he could talk! He seemed perfect for sales, but he was not selling. I met with him in his office to discuss his performance.

His desk was cluttered, but there was also evidence to suggest that he had been working. Piles of Post–It Notes, papers, contacting sheets, a few bids, and a box of tea bags made it nearly impossible to see his desktop.

After some small talk, I asked him about the forecasted numbers he had been assigned for the upcoming months. He was not certain that he could reach them. I knew that he was the type of salesperson who could easily be number one in his office, but he was not. The company expected that he was capable of producing better results, but they were on the verge of firing him.

They had asked me to help get his numbers up. I was given a stack of reports to review: his year–to–date numbers, his expense reports, his projections, and his customer list, to name a few. I briefly discussed the reports with him, but I focused more on the salesperson sitting across from me than on the numbers that represented him.

It did not take me long to realize that firing him would be a mistake. He had a lot of potential, but he was not living up to it. He was making phone calls, doing drop–bys, and scheduling presentations. He understood the various sales components, but was not able to pull it all together, which is not uncommon for many salespeople.

After thirty minutes of getting to know him and his business, I closed the report folders. The salesman looked at me expectantly, waiting for me to give him a definitive answer to his sales slump. Instead of giving him an answer, I asked, "Can I see your plan?" When he answered, "What plan?" I knew where the problem was.

I asked if he would hand me the box of tea bags from the corner of his desk. He quickly reached for it and handed it to me. I pointed to the back panel of the box and read the instructions to him:

1. Pour boiling water over tea bag
2. Brew for 3–5 minutes
3. Remove tea bag and stir
4. Add a lemon slice, honey, or milk

I asked him why there were detailed instructions on his desk about making tea but none about making money. He was silent, but he nodded his head slightly, which communicated volumes to me. There was evidence of great intentions on his desk, but not a single bullet point to help him achieve his sales goals. He not only understood my point, but he had received his answer. He needed a sales plan, a set of instructions to achieve 3–dimensional sales results.

I would like to say that his situation was unique, but it is all too common. Many salespeople have less substance in their sales plans, than the instructions to make a simple beverage. Isn't your business more valuable to you than a cup of tea?

I know that you see the benefit in gathering the information necessary to achieve better sales results. But without a plan, it will be difficult to see the path leading to success. Your plan will help you to know your clients, your rivals, your solutions, and your team. Yes, there is that much riding on your plan. So let's start putting it together to give you a 3–dimensional view of your sales operation.

Those who see the benefit of a sales plan often lack the skills to create an adequate plan. They may spend too much time preparing them. They may over–analyze and over–research, leaving little time to build their business. Your plan should be simple, concise, and easy to implement.

A sales plan is intended for two things:

1. Build your momentum to take action.
2. Keep you on track.

Your plan should never hamper your progress. Yes, you need to invest some time into putting it together, but no one ever said it had to be done during productive, business hours. If you want to be a success, one of the first things you need to learn is when to do certain tasks. You will not achieve 3–dimensional results with a nine–to–five work schedule. I typically develop and review my sales plan during times when clients are not available: either later in the evening or very early in the morning.

WHAT MAKES A SALES PLAN EFFECTIVE?

Before I started conducting coaching sessions, I had seen few salespeople with sales plans. The occasional plans I came across ranged from one paragraph of notes to thirty pages of detailed research. Some featured charts, graphs, and other impressive looking illustrations, but these plans did little to improve their sales. Some salespeople were proud of their sales plans, but were not proud of their sales results. Just having a plan is not enough. Anyone can make an eye–catching business plan by downloading a preformatted template from the internet.

The key is to know your plan. Identify the right information and use it to accelerate your results. I prefer a simple plan that is straight to the point.

Your plan needs to be flexible and easy to adapt to your selling environment.

A 3-dimensional sales plan includes the following:

- Your goals
- Your mission
- Your schedule
- Your projections
- Your results

YOUR GOALS

Becoming a 3-Dimensional Sales Leader is about coming full-circle in your career. Remember, Chapter 1 discussed turning your desires into sales goals. Now, your sales plan will begin with the goals you specified that will help you to increase your results. Assuming you have many important goals, where do you start? I start by listing each sales goal that I have, big and small. Then, I break them into two categories.

Two types of sales goals:

1. **Short-Term** – Goals that can be accomplished in less than 90 days
2. **Long-Term** – Goals that will require more than 90 days to accomplish

As you can imagine, you will focus first on accomplishing your short-term sales goals in your plan during the next 90 days. Accomplishing your short-term goals will provide you with the momentum and energy to keep moving toward your long-term sales goals. Your long-term goals will help to complete the big picture of your sales career. Both types of goals are important and both need to be accomplished. Your plan will make sure that you stay the course for both.

Many salespeople ask me what goals they should set. Everyone is different, but there is a common denominator that helps people to accomplish them: your sales goals must inspire you. They should be important enough that you will not give up. I have helped both new and seasoned salespeople to set goals.

Here are examples of goals that others have set. These may help to spark ideas for the goals you would like to accomplish. Modify them to fit your desires!

- Develop five new clients in 90 days
- Earn at least $10,000 per month
- Recruit ten new real estate agents
- Improve public speaking skills
- Expand business into three new states
- Open two new offices
- Set up three new corporate accounts
- Increase annual income to $250,000
- Give ten presentations per month
- Increase phone calls to twenty per day
- Attend three new networking events per month
- Complete three new sales per week
- Sell one new service to existing clients
- Give three large–group presentations

These are inspirational goals. Do your goals inspire you?

YOUR MISSION

Never forget your purpose. You should not only have a mission statement, but you should be deeply committed to it. Mission statements should be shared and understood by your team and your clients. The more people who know your mission statement, the more likely you are to honor it.

As a personal development coach, I follow the mission statement of my company, Think GREAT. Our mission statement is: *to help people to accomplish their goals, personal and professional, no matter what circumstances they face.* I believe in this mission statement with all of my heart. It is part of my plan, part of my life, and it always inspires me to do more.

What is your mission statement? Let it inspire you and make it an integral part of your plan.

YOUR SCHEDULE

Maximize each day. Each day is about 1% of your *90 Day Run*, so make it count. The success of your plan will depend on how well you are able to control your time. You cannot sell something yesterday. Today is all you have to work with – schedule it effectively!

Regardless of what you sell or whom you sell to, there are certain activities that need to be meticulously scheduled each day. The purpose of a schedule is to allow your plan to gain momentum, by keeping your actions on track. Life can throw many curve balls. Having a dedicated schedule will help you to keep hitting home runs in your business.

Your schedule will help to position you to complete more presentations and more sales if you focus on five key activities each day.

The 5 Key Activities:

1. Phone zone
2. Follow–up
3. Power lunches/dinners
4. Drop–bys
5. 3–dimensional activities

Phone Zone:

Phone zone is a specific block of time each day to call new and existing clients to set appointments. Do not let anything interfere with this golden time. Making contact is vital to your growth.

Follow–Up:

This activity is dedicated to providing necessary information to your prospects and clients. This is the time to return phone calls and e–mails. Do not attempt to mix this within your Phone Zone.

Power Lunches/Dinners:

Get face–to–face with prospects, new clients, and existing clients. Gather the information you need to better understand your clients and your competition. This is a great time to build and improve relationships.

Drop–Bys:

This is a powerful way to show your prospects and clients that you are committed to them. A drop–by says a lot about you, but they take time, especially when you do them consistently.

3–Dimensional Activities:

You will add new dimensions to your sales career as you attend after–hours events. Conventions, industry parties, mixers, and specific networking meetings are an excellent way to gain new important knowledge, and yes, to meet more people!

This is exactly what makes up my schedule. What does your schedule look like? Often, when I ask to see a salesperson's schedule, they show me their calendar. A calendar is not a schedule. A schedule is your guide to filling up your calendar with growth–related activities and appointments.

Most salespeople have an '8 and skate' mind set. They do their 8 hours for the day and then clock out, both physically and mentally. Your schedule will help to make sure that your plan takes on a life of its own. Without a dedicated, organized schedule, most salespeople fail to use their time constructively!

YOUR PROJECTIONS

Your plan should detail your projections for new business that you are expecting to earn. Your objective is to set solid projections for the upcoming week, the next month, and the year as a whole. If you are not on track to meet any of these projections, step up your efforts to fill in the gaps.

Seeing projections on a daily basis allows you to be more excited about each upcoming day. If you are unable to forecast new business for specific time periods, increase your sense of urgency and schedule more activities in your calendar.

You may not always be able to predict what business will come in, but you can certainly get a better understanding of what to expect by updating and keeping a close eye on your projections.

YOUR RESULTS

When you think about it, every salesperson wants to go from point 'A' (their important goals) to point 'B' (their desired results). Each action in between needs to support that process. Focusing on too many steps may cause them to get off track and waste precious time.

At the end of the day, your results will give you a confirmation of how well your sales gears are performing. Did your phone calls turn into appointments? Did your appointments turn into new business? Did the referrals you received turn into new clients? Did you achieve the 3–dimensional sales results you were striving for?

You should get into the habit of constantly reviewing and updating your sales results. Tracking your results will allow you to make the necessary adjustments to your performance. If your sales business is not growing, it is dying. Your plan will make sure that your sales pulse remains strong and that your career does not flat–line.

90 DAY RUN

To maximize the effectiveness of your plan, you should operate within a 90 Day Run. Succesful salespeople target a specified date range to operate in. I have reviewed plans that map out a one-month period to accomplish sales goals, while others have a five-year time frame.

For your plan to be effective, it must have definitive time parameters. I use the power of a *90 Day Run* as the foundation for my sales plans. This is a concept I discuss in great detail in my book, *The GOAL Formula*. I have found that people have the ability to stay focused for about 90 days. In fact, they can change more than their business during that time period, they can change their lives.

I discovered this benefit firsthand, when I was eighteen years old. I stepped off of the bus at the Marine Corps Recruiting Depot in San Diego, California, as a raw recruit. Ninety days later I marched across the parade deck and graduated with my platoon as a U.S. Marine. The steps between our goals and our results were planned out with precise detail. Our drill instructors harnessed the power of a ninety-day plan to transform a group of undisciplined civilians into hard-charging Marines.

What could you do in 90 days? By operating within 90 day blocks of time, your plan will transform your sales efforts into 3-dimensional sales results. I have used 90 Day Runs to reach my objectives in the military, the financial services industry, and the entertainment industry. Now, as a sales coach, I use this concept to train salespeople from all industries to achieve their desired results.

By setting up your plan within a *90 Day Run*, you can course-correct as needed, develop beneficial habits, eliminate bad habits, and stay on track with your actions as you pursue your results. As you develop your plan, I recommend that you share it with as many people as you can. The more people who know about your plan, the more likely you will stick with it. Do not treat your plan like a top-secret document, keeping it away from everyone. Instead, enlist the support of people you know, and they will help to sustain your efforts. No one does it alone.

In the financial services industry, I used *90 Day Runs* to stay focused on my plan. It allowed me to become a top producer, recruiter, and trainer. In the entertainment industry, I utilized back-to-back *90 Day Runs* with my entire sales team to bring our sales plan to life. We not only accomplished our goals, but we increased the annual sales production by nearly 300%.

The question is not, "Does a *90 Day Run* work?" The question is, "Will you use a *90 Day Run* for your plan?" The next 90 days are coming. What are you going to do with them?

If you want your sales performance to improve, then work your plan! Your plan will not only help you to stay on track with your goals, it will separate you from your competition and will help to complete your transformation into a 3-Dimensional Sales Leader.

AFTERWORD

A New Perspective of an Old Profession

Change your perception of selling and experience new levels of success.

As a sales trainer, I have been blessed to speak with thousands of sales professionals in a wide array of industries. I am always honored when they ask me about improving their performance. And I feel fortunate that I can provide answers that will truly benefit them.

Regardless of what products people sell, one of the most common questions I am asked is, "What's the one thing I can do to increase my sales?" This is a great question because it allows me to address one of the most significant obstacles in sales today. Many salespeople hope that there is one specific tip that will improve their results. They often invest much valuable time searching for the elusive secret of sales but fail to discover the 3–dimensional answer that will enable them to achieve the success they desire.

The one thing you can do to enhance your results is to stop thinking that there is just one thing. However, while there is not *one* thing needed to succeed in sales, there is a *first* thing! Change your perception of selling and your clients' perception of buying. By changing the perception of what sales means, you have a fighting chance to experience new levels of success.

Beyond that, effective selling is achieved by systematically blending all of the sales elements that this book discusses. *Desire, Determination*, and *Decisions* will fuel the *5 Sales Gears* that you consistently turn, supported by the *3-Dimensional Sales Knowledge* you need to acquire, build upon and maintain.

Your sales machine will function like a fine-tuned vehicle, capable of taking you to any destination. Becoming a 3-Dimensional Sales Leader allows you to have a vehicle that is fully loaded, with all the options to make it a smoother ride. But never forget that your sales vehicle is not intended to take you for a ride by yourself. Your clients ride shotgun. After all, they also have a destination to get to.

As your sales machine continues to take you and your career in new and exciting directions, paying careful attention to your perception of selling will open up new opportunities.

Now it is time to introduce the new you to the buyers of the world. Why would they stay with their 1-dimensional salesperson or 2-dimensional sales professional, when they can now choose a 3-Dimensional Sales Leader?

Fasten your seat belts, check your mirrors, and put on your 3-D glasses! Your new sales journey starts now!

ABOUT THE AUTHOR

ERIK THERWANGER

Erik Therwanger began his unique career by serving in the U.S. Marine Corps. Leadership, honor, and integrity did not end after his four year tour of duty; they became the foundation of his life, both personally and professionally.

After receiving the news that his wife had been diagnosed with cancer, Erik left his job in the entertainment industry, became her caregiver, and started his new career in sales. With no formal training, he began selling financial services. Relying on the strategies and techniques he learned as a Marine, he quickly became a top producer, recruiter, and trainer.

Erik's passion for helping others led to the creation of Think GREAT®. He successfully blended his leadership skills, his unparalleled ability to inspire and develop teams, and his wide-array of sales experience, to provide practical solutions to individuals and organizations.

Sharing his personal story and elite strategies, Erik inspires audiences to strive for new levels of greatness. His interactive and powerful workshops highlight his step-by-step process for increasing results: The Trifecta of Growth™. Erik delivers a compelling message that leaves a lasting impact on organizations, creating the necessary momentum to develop strong leaders, build visionary teams, and elevate sales results.

As the author of the Think GREAT® Collection, Erik has combined his challenging life experiences with his goal–setting techniques, to provide proven strategies to enhance the lives of others.

As part of his greater purpose, Erik dedicates time to helping in the fight against cancer by working with the Relay For Life and serving as a Legislative Ambassador with the American Cancer Society.

Erik is also the founder of 4–Star Speakers, an elite group of motivational speakers, representing the four branches of the armed services.

LLC, Agoura Hills, California

WWW.THINKGREAT90.COM

Please visit our website for additional information to help you and your organization achieve greater results:

- Powerful Products
- Inspirational Seminars
- Interactive Tools
- Events and Appearances with Erik Therwanger
- Register for FREE Resources
- News, blog, and forum

To order additional information, please visit

http://www.thinkgreat90.com

More books coming soon in the Think GREAT® Collection:

- **A Caregiver's Orders**

- **The Scale Factor**

- **TRUE Leadership**

- **Visionary Team Building**

- **Your Financial Toolbox**

- ***Goal Planning Strategy (G.P.S.) Workbook***

Made in the USA
Lexington, KY
03 July 2017